The Wrappings and the Gifts

Answers to questions about life, purpose, immortality, and the spirit.

by Richard M. Eyre

ISBN 1-55517-303-9

PREFACE

We live in a world that seems to have more questions than answers, more seekers than finders. We yearn, perhaps more than any other people of any other time, for a clearer picture of who we are and how we fit into the universe. We're driven to improve ourselves not only physically and mentally but *spiritually*. We sense that there is more to life, and more to *us*, than the humdrum routine and the social and economic competition of the day-to-day.

We flock to the high-held hope of *self-help* but ultimately find it to be an oxymoron. We feel the need for help from something other than ourselves, from someone higher than ourselves.

We're drawn to the "spiritual" but not to the "religious" so the other-world glimpses or feelings we do discover are isolated, disconnected, incomplete, like single pieces of a puzzle. We long for continuity — for answers that "ring true" to our hearts as well as our minds, and for the interlocking pieces that can give us a full picture of where we came from, why we are here, and where we are going.

We know, deep within ourselves, that the real answers have to do with God and with our relationship to Him.

Yet for so many, churches seem out of touch and irrelevant. And many who go to church, while they find some peace and solace, wish for a more specific and more complete picture of their own eternal nature and of the purpose, plan, and persona of God.

As I write books or give lectures around the world on values, on balance, on families, I find people and audiences everywhere who want more than philosophies, techniques, and self-help formulas. They want spiritual insight, they want answers about eternal purpose, about immortality and about the mind and will of God. These answers do not come from gurus or motivators or best-selling authors. Questions of the spirit require answers from the spirit — answers that have to do more with soulful enlightenment than with secular education, more to do with inspiration than with intellect.

I believe I have found these spiritual answers — not deduced them or developed them — *found* them, in the theology of a religion that is unlike any other. For years as I have spoken or written to "secular" audiences, I've felt the frustration of giving the "self-help" part of the answer but not the higher "spiritual help" part. I've felt like I was leading people to a plateau rather than a mountaintop, dealing more with the short term than the long, more with the symptoms than the cause, more with the mind than with the soul.

Well, I don't want to do that anymore. I want at least to *offer*, especially to those who have read my other books or heard my secular lecturing, the deeper answers, the bigger picture, the things I believe were not thought up by men but revealed by God.

FOREWORD

When I was nineteen years old I got on a train in Salt Lake City and went to New York City as a full-time, unpaid, voluntary missionary for The Church of Jesus Christ of Latter-day Saints (nicknamed "Mormon"). During the next two years, I discovered that what I was telling people was practical as well as true, and I watched the teaching of the Church, the answers of Christ's Gospel, and the programs of His Church change the hearts and the lives of individuals and families. When my "mission" was over, I returned to college, finished my education at the Harvard Business School and began a management consulting career.

Five years later, in the midst of building a national consulting company, the Church called me to be a "Mission President" in London, England — to be in charge of a rotating group of over two hundred young missionaries for three years. There was no pay, but our belief in the Church and what it could do for people compelled Linda and me to go. We brought four young children with us, and two more were born while we were there.

It was the most marvelous experience of our lives. I got up every morning knowing that what I would do (and what our missionaries would do) that day could genuinely help people, enhance their family and spiritual lives and add to their happiness. There were no ulterior motives or hidden agendas. We were there to share and to give.

During that first period of time in England (we have been back frequently since and think of London now as a second home) we formed many friendships, one of the most lasting of which was with a member of the British Parliament who I will call Graham. Graham and I shared similar political and economic views and we also shared a penchant for and an enjoyment in discussing spiritual subjects (although we found much less time to do so than we would have liked).

The time flew by and before I knew it, our term of voluntary service and missionary work was over and we returned to the U.S. It was hard to leave because there was much unfinished business and many unfinished friendships. I stayed in touch with Graham, and some of my letters to him, particularly one very long one, are the basic substance of this book. I called the long letter "The Wrappings and the Gifts," and it appears here exactly as it was sent to Graham. The earlier letters and communication represented in this book condense a combination of discussions and correspondence I've had with Graham and with others.

The last time Graham and I spoke before we left England the first time, he said he'd like to know more about the spiritual beliefs that motivated me to leave my career and my other interests for three years. He said he didn't want an answer right then, and didn't want an answer by phone — he wanted a real letter — something he could ponder and think about. A month or so later he sent me a note to remind me to write and in it he commented again on his admiration for my church and for the effect he had seen it have on the everyday lives of people. I wrote back to him with what I'll call letter #1.

Letter #1

Dear Graham:

Thanks for your note and for your ongoing interest in the spiritual things we've discussed (too briefly) over the last several months. I'm sure I've learned as much or more than you from our conversations. I particularly liked your metaphor about the "spiritual circuitry" that surrounds us always and our opportunity to "plug into it" and get impressions and guidance and spiritual perspective and energy whenever we are willing and humble enough.

With regard to my church, I agree with your allusion to its "practicality and pragmatism." It really is more of a way of life than it is a place to go on Sunday.

Some particulars:

1. **Youth programs**: As you have observed, Mormon kids are really *involved*. Scouting programs and organized athletic, music and drama activities keep church buildings busy nearly every night of the week.

2. **Lay ministry**: Since there are no paid ministers, the local "Bishop" (head of the local congregation) might be a doctor, or an architect, or a plumber; and virtually everyone is involved in some "church job" . . . teaching a class, directing a play, coaching a team, visiting those in need, etc. It is, as you mentioned, a classic example of everyone helping each other. It's not as insular as you might think, however. A lot of the "church jobs" involve service in the broader community.

3. **Welfare program**: Mormons don't generally need or use any form of state assistance because the church's welfare program works so well. Groups of congregations operate volunteer-staffed farms, factories, etc. which produce basic necessities. People who are between jobs can

work in these facilities and earn "credits" with which they can "buy" basic necessities. The church also has job training and job placement programs for members.

4. **Health**: Our belief that the body is the "temple" for the spirit is at the root of the health code that has existed since the earliest days of the church. Abstinence from alcohol and tobacco as well as coffee and tea along with an emphasis on exercise and natural foods has made Mormons a remarkably healthy people. Abstinence is also the operative moral code regarding premarital sex — not only for health concerns but because of our belief in the sanctity and the beauty of the marriage commitment.

5. **Families**: The church gives *huge* help to parents and families. It provides materials and guidelines for a "family home evening" once a week designed to improve communication and commitment with each other. The church sponsors frequent family activities, marriage and parenting classes, and all sorts of other efforts to strengthen family life.

6. **Missionary system**: Young men and young women have the opportunity around the age of twenty to spend eighteen months to two years in full-time voluntary service. They are "called" to some part of the world (over fifty thousand are now serving in more than one hundred and thirty countries) where they give service, strengthen families, and tell others about their beliefs. They return home, fluent in languages and cultures and usually with a clearer idea of their own educational and career goals. Retired people (as individuals or couples) also go throughout the world as missionaries — thus staying more active and involved than they would otherwise be.

Graham, there is so much more that I could mention in this vein — humanitarian projects, educational opportun-

ities, neighborhood and community involvement — suffice it
to say that ours is a hugely *active* and *involved* and *involving* church. But I don't want to go beyond what you want
to know. Write when you can and let me know what kind of
further interest you have.

All the best,
Richard

*Well, Graham did have further interest, and he was a
little impatient with my letter. He told me that I was covering
things he already knew — that his observations of the* practicality *of the church, of how involved it was in people's everyday life — were the very* reasons *that he wanted to know more
. . . not about the* programs *of the church, but about its*
doctrines.

*Could I please write back, he wondered, and this time tell
him something that would help him understand* why *Mormons
were the way they were. "What do you* believe, *" he said,
"that makes you what you are? What is* behind *and* beneath
*the kind of people you are. What separates you doctrinally
from other Christian faiths?"*

*"What separates us . . . doctrinally . . . from other
Christian faiths?" I thought about his question for several
days and then wrote letter #2.*

Letter #2

Dear Graham:

I hope all is well with you and yours. And I welcome the opportunity of trying to go a little further with our discussion about my church or, as I would say, about Christ's church, and therein lies the start of my answer. I believe it is actually Christ's own church.

In fact, Graham, the full name of the church is really the key to what I want to say in this letter, "*The Church of Jesus Christ of Latter-day Saints.*" *Mormon,* as you know, is only a nickname — and somewhat of an unfortunate one, I think, because it often prevents the real name — which says so much about what we believe — from being used. ("Mormon" as I think you know, comes from the *Book of Mormon* — an ancient book of scripture originating in the Americas that we use *with* the *Holy Bible.* I'll get back to this book later.)

But ponder the church's real name, because it says so much. "The Church of Jesus Christ of Latter-day Saints." I believe that Christ's original church — The Church of Jesus Christ of *Former*-day Saints — was established by the Lord, complete with a priesthood of deacons, teachers, evangelists, etc. as outlined in the *Bible* to safeguard His doctrines and to perpetuate the way of life that He taught. "Saints" was the Biblical name for members of His church. The twelve apostles were His church's leading authorities next to Himself. They were to maintain unity and to delegate priesthood authority to the Bishops of local congregations. When an apostle died, as illustrated in the first chapter of Acts, the other eleven met together and by inspiration chose a replacement.

But after Christ's crucifixion, as the persecution of His church escalated, the Apostles (who were scattered and out of touch with each other) were killed, leaving no one to ordain lesser priesthood officers or to maintain the purity of Christ's doctrine. The apostolic "link" between God in Heaven and His church on earth was gone. Divisions and doctrinal disputes resulted and the priesthood or power of God vested in men died with the death of those who had received it from the Apostles. Doctrines were diluted, changed, compromised on. Constantine exacerbated the problem by making Christianity the official church of Rome and politicizing all aspects of it.

From then through the Dark Ages, Christ's church and its teachings were progressively changed and corrupted. Finally the courageous men that we call reformers broke away from the Catholic Church, attempting to find and renew the old truths, and started the protestant reformation. Significantly, none of the major reformers — Luther, Calvin, Wesley, Williams — sought to form their own church or a new church. They wanted to *reform* the existing church. Furthermore, they recognized their own lack of Christ's true authority and indicated that they were awaiting a *restoration* in which God himself would restore what had been lost.

Graham, I believe the *reformation* prepared the way and set the stage for a *restoration* that took place in the early 1800s through a boy prophet named Joseph Smith. Young Joseph was not a reformer or a learned man. He was an honest seeker who was used by God (in the same pattern that all biblical prophets were used) to restore truth and light to the earth. The whole *Bible*, in fact, is a series of "dispensations" . . . truth being lost from the earth and then being restored again through a chosen prophet. Why would God's pattern change?

The restoration through Joseph Smith was a remarkable thing. Illuminating truths about God, about man, and about God's relationship to man were returned to earth — restored by angels and by God himself. God's plan for mankind's progress and salvation was restored. Much of the enlightenment came through an ancient record called *The Book of Mormon* which told of Christ's post-resurrection visit to the Americas — a book that complements, supplements, clarifies and expands the *Holy Bible*. God's true priesthood was restored and once again Christ's full church, complete with Apostles and all other priesthood offices was re-established. Hence the name *The Church of Jesus Christ of Latter-day Saints*.

Graham, the practicality and relevance of this church is not an accident. The fact that it is the fastest-growing church on earth is not a coincidence. It is the very church of Christ, and while all Christian churches carry the most important of all truths — that Christ is our Divine Savior — *this* church, His own restored church, is complete and carries *all* of the truths necessary to make sense of this life and to make a meaningful pursuit of happiness.

May you, through *your* pursuit, find this to be so.

Sincerely, Richard

It wasn't that Graham didn't like letter #2. It just wasn't what he was asking for. His return correspondence made that clear. He thanked me for the overview of Christian history and the apostasy and for my "logical-sounding" claim that a restoration had to follow the reformation. But he was blunt in saying that it did not help him with the personal questions and doubts he had. All his life, he said, he had tried to reconcile his faith with the inconsistencies and cruelties of life. He was deeply troubled by the huge inequalities and injustices in our world, by the bad things that happen to good people, by the huge percentages of humanity who would never hear of Christ and the things He taught. He wanted desperately to understand the spiritual promptings and frequent feelings of deja vu that came to him. He felt sure there was a world beyond this one and a spiritual reality but he could not define it or make sense of it.

Could I please, he asked, get to the root of what I believed and share with him the real source and essence of my own faith — not the wrappings but the gifts.

The next day I wrote letter #3.

Letter #3

Dear Graham:

Thanks so much for your last correspondence and its invitation to express more of *what* was restored. I'm still hesitant to try to do so by letter. Personal, face-to-face visits with our missionaries, young and inexperienced as they are, is the best way to approach and receive these things. (Actually, it is the best way *because* of their youth and inexperience. They won't convince you of anything so if you believe, you'll know it's because of the Spirit and not because of the missionaries.) While you're deciding whether you want to take that step, let me pose to you eleven "what if" questions. I think you'll agree that *if* they are true, *then* there may exist real answers for the difficult questions you pose about the human condition.

WHAT IF . . .

1. What if . . .
We, each of us, lived before this life, not inside another person or as something else but in another place as our-selves? Our deja vu and sense that we have deeper and older selves is accurate. We were spirit individuals before we were born.

2. What if . . .
The fatherhood of God is more than a metaphor? We are His spiritual children. He is an all powerful being of spirit and body and we are His offspring in His image.

3. What if . . .
This earth was designed and created for us — a limitless-option school where experience could expand and *enhance* our awareness, our potential and our joy, allowing

us to become more like our Heavenly Father in comprehension and in capacity? His "commandments" are the
happiest ways to live — they are loving counsel from a wise
father.

4. What if . . .

We are here on earth not so much to find comfort or
fulfillment as to *learn*? Mortality is part of a much longer
journey and first time experiences like a physical body and
parenthood of our spirit brothers and sisters are part of our
eternal education and part of God's eternal plan. Families,
formed here, will become the basis of God's eternal organization. Circumstances that may appear arbitrary and unfair
will make more sense in an eternal perspective.

5. What if . . .

As spirits within bodies, we are still capable of receiving
light and insight but with specific memory of our premortal
life blotted out so agency and choice can exist? Through
prophets, church, and individual inspiration, spiritual
answers are available, but only as we ask and listen.

6. What if . . .

As spirits within physical bodies we are still close to the
spiritual world, and it is close to us? Other spirits who have
departed this life or not yet come can sometimes be felt
nearby, and our Heavenly Father's spirit guides our lives
and answers our prayers.

7. What if . . .

Relationships and what we have learned (and become)
are the two things we can take with us into the after life —
an after life where we will judge ourselves and be with God
if we are comfortable in His presence?

8. What if . . .

Those who have no opportunity to hear of this eternal
plan receive that chance in the spirit world that follows so

that *all* have a fair and equal opportunity to accept and follow it or to reject it?

9. What if . . .

Our eldest spiritual sibling helped create this world with His Father (and our Father), guided its destiny as the God of the Old Testament, and came to live on this earth and redeem its people as Jesus Christ? He had no earthly father and, as God's only begotten son, without sin, had power to lay down His life and take it up again. This He did, in agony, mercy, and sacrifice, paying for our sins that we too might resurrect and return to God.

10. What if . . .

The spirit and the body constitute the complete soul of man? Physical bodies enhance our joy and increase our ability to comprehend and benefit from the temporal universe and grow to be more like our Father.

11. What if . . .

God's word and will comes to this earth through prophets, but in deference to our agency and mortality's purpose (of growth and self-determination), is not required or enforced? When truth is lost or distorted by apostasy or misinterpretation, God restores it through new prophets so that truth seekers, if they are diligent and prayerful, can always find it.

THEN . . .

There may be reasons and explanations for your questions about:

1. The seemingly random unfairness of life and the bad things that happen to good people.

2. Feelings of deja vu, flashes of unexpected but exceptionally clear insight, and a sense of "remembering" as we learn.

3. Impressions of closeness to people long gone or deep longings and emotions that seem beyond the things of daily life.

4. Our natural assumptions and feelings that life and love continue after death.

5. The incredible and often disturbing variety of life — the intensity and "extremeness" of both the good and the bad.

6. Why some hear and know of Christ and His gospel on this earth and others do not.

Graham, I'm not trying to be illusive or indirect. I Just want you to ponder the possibility of some of these things before I (or preferably two of our young missionaries) present fuller explanations.

> With love and best wishes,
> Richard

The whole tone of Graham's return correspondence was different.

"Now we're getting somewhere," he said. "You're finally understanding my question. I'm not asking about the practical results *of your church (your letter #1). If I hadn't known about those I'd not have been curious in the first place. And I'm not asking about the* process *by which the church was restored and established (your letter #2). While the claim that God and angels re-visited the earth is exciting (and certainly intellectually challenging), it's not how the parcel is wrapped and delivered that interests me most — it's what was* inside. What *was restored . . . what doctrines, what insights, what understanding? What was restored that will help me make more sense of my life and of life in general? Your letter #3 began to get at it — but in an almost teasing, hypothetical way. It's those answers I want — as direct and complete as you can give them to me. Don't ask me questions . . . or give me answers in the form of questions. Tell me what was restored. Tell me what is inside the box."*

Finally I understand what Graham was really asking about. He wanted to know the content *of the restoration. I decided to use his own metaphor to write letter #4 — a much longer letter not about the "wrappings" but about the "gifts." In the letter (which comprises the balance of this book), I made no reference to the source or the* how *or to the circumstances under which the truths were restored. In other words, I ignored the "wrappings" and talked only of the "gifts," feeling more and more as I wrote that each gift carried with it its own independent ring of truth and needed no "proof" or "evidence" to be believed. It needed only a sincere and spiritual reader.*

I wrote letter #4 in the mountains, parts of it on long horse rides alone where I pondered Graham's questions as I climbed sagebrush ridges or passed beneath giant firs. When a "gift" became isolated and clear in my mind, I hobbled my horse, found a rock or a log to sit on, took out my paper and wrote it down. Then I rode on, trying to grasp and conceptualize the next gift.

The Wrappings and the Gifts

An open letter overviewing
the distinctive doctrines
of the Restored Gospel of Christ

Letter #4:
THE WRAPPINGS AND THE GIFTS

**An open letter overviewing the
distinctive doctrines of the restored Gospel**

*And a metaphor about how we sometimes become so
infatuated and occupied with a package's wrappings (the
miraculous visions and the process of restoration) that we fail
to fully see or appreciate the gifts inside (the actual truths,
insights, and understandings about God and man that were
restored).*

TABLE OF CONTENTS

Letter: the Gifts

Dear Graham:

Thanks for your last correspondence. I think I truly understand (finally) what you are asking me and I will try to be both more to the point and more detailed in this letter.

I will use your metaphor — the one suggesting that I get to *what* was contained in the "package" of the restoration rather than dealing with the wrappings and bows of *how* it was restored.

Let me begin by expanding and personalizing that metaphor a bit. In our family, as I suppose is the case in most, we look forward to the first birthday of each child and to the first Christmas following that birthday — we long to give gifts to these little ones and we are anxious for them to be old enough to celebrate with us, to open presents and to feel our love as they enjoy what is inside.

But on these first holidays a fairly predictable and somewhat frustrating thing occurs: Our tiny children become preoccupied with the wrappings and the bows. The crinkly paper and the bright colors fascinate them and so fully capture their attention that they never get to what's inside, or if they do get to it, the gift isn't flashy enough (or perhaps requires too much concentration) to take their minds off the spectacular wrappings.

The gifts of the restored Church of Jesus Christ of Latter-day Saints are insights and truths about the nature and purposes of man, about the reality and the plan of God and about the relationship of men to God and the inter-relationships between His plan and our purpose. The gifts are also His power and His peace and His ways, transformed to our voltage and available for our use.

The wrappings and the packaging are the circumstances and the people and the methods through which these truths

were restored. The eye-and mind-catching wrapping paper
includes a historical and scriptural record inscribed on
sheets of gold. The spectacular ribbons and bows include
revelations, modern day prophets and visitations and restorations by angelic messengers.

No wonder so many become preoccupied with the
wrappings and fail to see beyond them to the gifts. No
wonder so relatively few know of the inner insights of the
gifts and so relatively many know about the outer appearance of the package.

This is not to say that the "wrappings" are unimportant.
Indeed, the *way* in which things were restored reveals truth
about the "unchangeable-ness" and impartiality of God and
of His methods, reassuring us that He loves us as much and
deals with us as personally as He did with those of old.

But for so many people the packaging is so bright, so
extraordinary, so outside the realm of their normal experience, that they dwell on it and either fail to look at the gifts
inside or see them with a blurred or prejudiced perspective
because of the wrappings they come in.

What I hope to do in this letter, Graham, is to reverse
the usual sequence and order of things . . . to start off *inside*
the package . . . to focus on the gifts, paying attention to the
wrappings only after the gifts themselves are perceived, and
appreciated, and enjoyed.

The gifts are answers, insights and powers. They enable
men not only to understand their lives better . . . but to *live*
them better. They are not new answers, but very old ones . . .
insights that have always been part of God's revealed word
to man, lost from the earth in times of apostasy, confusion
and compromise — then recovered and restored in times of
freedom and faith.

The word *restore* is the key. Please remember that a
restoration is fundamentally different than a *reformation*.

In a reformation the initiative comes from man — a restoration must be at God's initiative. The courageous reformers dared to acknowledge the contradictions and discrepancies of the altered Christianity that emerged from the Dark Ages. They elevated the minds of men and prepared the world for the restoration of the plain and precious parts of Christ's gospel which had been lost. This letter is a listing of some of the gifts of that restoration:

You will quickly see that I have not tried to "present" the gifts of the restoration in an evidential or "selling" tone. Nor have I tried to back up every point with a biblical scripture or some form of evidence or "proof." Rather, I've tried to simply *state* these gifts in the most simple and straight-forward manner.

I've taken this approach for two reasons: 1. My purpose is not to "win you over" or to convince or compel you to agree with or accept each point — rather, it is simply to share with you, as my friend, the most precious insights I possess. 2. I believe (we both do, as we have often discussed) that truth carries its own "ring." When truth is stated plainly, and when it is heard (or read) by one who listens without bias and who trusts his own feelings — then it needs no back up, no foot notes, no debate — it rings true in the heart and mind, and it stands alone for itself.

Gift 1: Knowledge of Man's Pre-mortal Existence and of the Eternal Fatherhood of God.

> Our birth is but a sleep and a forgetting.
> The soul that rises with us, our life's star
> hath had elsewhere its setting
> and cometh from afar—
> not in complete forgetfulness,
> and not in entire nakedness,
> but trailing clouds of glory do we come
> from God who is our home.
> — Wordsworth

Your great English Poet Laureate William Wordsworth (whose home on Lake Windermere we visited two weeks before leaving England) is not the only one who believes that each man's spirit existed in another place (with God) before his birth into mortality; although he may be the only one to have ever stated it with such haunting beauty.

Many people believe they lived before birth because of personal experiences of deja vu . . . or because of things they seem to know that they don't remember having ever learned . . . or simply because, in their deeper moments, they feel there is more to them than the sparse accumulation of a few years of earthly experience.

The Bible makes several references to man's pre-mortal life, including God's statement to Jeremiah that He knew him *before* He had formed him "in the belly" and "before he came forth out of the womb." (Jer. 1:5)

Irrespective of how many people believe it or how many scriptures refer to it, no Catholic or Protestant

church teaches or officially holds a belief in the
pre-mortal life of man. All teach of some form of life
after death, but theirs is a concept of "one way eternity"
because it couples with the doctrine that individual
humans flare into existence at the time of their birth. The
only exception is the *restored* Church of Jesus Christ
which offers the knowledge of a pre-existence as one of
its gifts.

Knowledge of a pre-mortal life answers the question
"Where did I come from?" and allows man to approach
the successive questions of "Why am I here?" and
"Where am I going?" And it gives a perspective that
allows us to deal with the seemingly random vicissitudes
of life.

Prior to our life here, prior even to the existence of
this earth, we lived as spirit sons and daughters of God.
We were separate and individual, even as we are now.
Our Heavenly Father's goal, then as now, was our
progress and happiness. Over the eons of time that we
lived with our Father, we learned and grew —
progressing not by changing our identities or taking on
other life forms, but by moving through different types of
challenge, different realms of experience.

The first-born spirit and thus our eldest spirit brother
was Jehovah. Another leader and older brother in God's
family was Lucifer.

There came a time in the course of our "eternal
progression" when the element of complete agency and
individual choice was prerequisite to further growth. We
needed the challenges and tempering of a physical
existence in a realm of finite time; and we required the
stretching, deepening experience of becoming parents

ourselves in order to understand and more closely resemble God, *our* parent.

For these purposes God conceived a temporal earth, bounded by time and by a finite span of physical years where we would receive, for the first time in eternity, the power of procreation and the opportunity to operate and to discipline appetite-laden physical bodies of flesh and bone.

Lucifer, possibly through an inadequate understanding of the need for agency but more probably through his interest in recognition and power, proposed an existence of mandatory obedience and processed experience in which his control would insure that none would be allowed to make mistakes that would jeopardize their return to God.

Opposing him was Jehovah who defended and articulated the Father's plan of agency wherein each individual could progress according to his own decisions, discipline and direction, wherein each would have the opportunity to fail as well as to succeed and whereby mortals could make independent choices through which they could advance themselves even as they glorified their Father.

Two-thirds of the hosts of Heaven followed Jehovah and the Father, becoming participants in mortality. One-third followed Lucifer and were cast out, creating a force of opposition which, ironically, was an essential part of a plan of agency.

Knowing of these "beginnings" gives us a perspective and a framework in which to view life's circumstances as well as life's purposes. Knowing where we came from is essential in understanding why we are here. These insights are one of the great gifts of the restoration.

Gift 2: Knowledge of the Purposes of Earth and Mortality

Understanding God as a personal and loving Father, and knowing of our pre-life with Him gives us access to a simple comparison that helps to make the purposes of earth and mortality more understandable and clear: Just as a wise earthly father recognizes that there comes a time when his children must have independence and separation from him in order to find themselves and become competent and separate entities, so our Heavenly Father recognized that our progress required an independent sphere with endless options of choice and without the coercion of a Lucifer-proposed dictatorship or the direction of a complete memory of our earlier life.

As we are born into mortality, a veil of forgetfulness shrouds our minds, blocking memory of our previous life with God and creating the opportunity both for faith and for independent choice. The veil is something of a "semi-permeable membrane" however, because certain deep feelings, an inherent "conscience" or sense of values, and some of the "clouds of glory" spoken of by Wordsworth manage to linger in our memory even in our state of forgetfulness.

People, then, are eternal. Eternity exists, for each of us in both directions — forward and backward. Endlessness in either direction is hard for our mortal, finite, time-bound minds to comprehend, but we have always lived, and earth life is only one phase in our existence, one grade in school. Our Father, Heavenly Father, sent us here — away to this earthly school — with His blessings, and with His hopes that we would return wiser for our experience, more free because of our practice in exercising agency, and more like Him because of our progress and development and because of our own parenthood.

Earth can accurately be called a test, but it is well to remember that it is not God who needs to test us but we who need to test ourselves. It is not enough for God to know us and to know the choices we would make. We must know ourselves and must actually make our own choices.

Physical bodies which may seem, because of their frailty, more of an impediment than an opportunity, are in fact an incredible blessing. Our bodies expand our range of feelings and experience. They afford us the previously unobtainable privilege of procreation and the physical expression of love. They allow us to learn to deal with and handle the physical world as well as to observe it and appreciate its metaphors and lessons as well as its dramatic beauty. Indeed, when our opportunity to gain a physical body and come to a physical earth was first announced to us, scripture tells us that we "shouted for joy."

And our joy, as we are told elsewhere in scripture is the very purpose for mortality.

"Adam fell that men might be (mortal) and men are (mortal) that they might have joy."

"Joy" in this context means much more than mere pleasure, amusement, or passing happiness. Rather, the purpose of life is to discover and appreciate the joy of self-determination, of accepting and being equal to difficult challenges, of loving the beauty of body and earth, of creating families and forming deep relationships, of struggling and searching for temporal as well as spiritual truth, and of looking for and finding God through faith that is stronger than the veil.

As we have often discussed in other contexts, Graham, there is *power in purpose*. Deep insights into the purpose of mortal life is a powerful and valuable gift of the restoration.

Gift 3: Knowledge of the Degrees and Dimensions of Life After Death

The simplistic (and with analysis *terrifying*) doctrine of an arbitrary, two-option hereafter consisting of an "eternal rest" *heaven* or an "eternal burning" *hell* is neither satisfying nor in any way comforting to the seeking mind. One of the gifts of the restoration is a view of after-life that is not only clearer but also more logical, more fair, more motivational, and more beautiful.

Just as physical birth is the taking on of a physical body by the spirit, physical death is the separation of spirit and body. The spirits of all men and women, upon death, go to a place of light called the Spirit World where they await a universal resurrection, which will occur at a later time and which is the reuniting of the spirit with a perfected but still tangible physical body.

In the spirit world we remain ourselves and retain our characteristics and thought processes in a spiritual form, absent from our physical bodies. Many of the teachings of Christ's restored Gospel — about a place of warming light where we recognize other departed beings and review our mortal lives — have had an interesting sort of "verification" in the recent international best-selling books like Betty J. Eadie's *Embraced by the Light* or in *Life After Life* where author Raymond Moody presents hundreds of case studies of "near death experiences" where people left their bodies and were transported into a realm of light, met beings of light, and were able to view (or review) their earth exper-ience. Dr. Moody calls Mormons "the most prominent of the Western religions to . . . accept near death experiences and the notion of a doorway to a spiritual world." He indicates that Mormon feelings on the transcendence of the spirit are in keeping with his research and questioning of those who experienced near death and recalled leaving their bodies.

In the Spirit World, those who have never had the opportunity to learn accurate truth about God and His plan are afforded that opportunity. Indeed, as Peter tells us in I Peter 3:18-19 and 4:6, Christ himself went to the spirit world after His death to teach those who lived during a time of universal wickedness (Noah's time) and thus had no opportunity to accept and live by true principles.

Only when all men have had equal opportunity to accept God and Christ and their way of life will the judgment and universal resurrection occur. The judgment will have elements of a self-judgment in that we will gravitate to the level and to the people wherein and with whom we are most comfortable. If we have made wise decisions and learned to live by God-like principles we will return to live with God. If our life styles and associations find more commonality and comfortableness in levels below God, then we will place ourselves in those lower levels.

The apostle Paul spoke of three main "degrees of glory" or places where resurrected beings would live, the highest of the three being the place where God and Christ dwell. But Paul also made it clear, as does the restored Church, that within these three levels there will be an infinite number of rewards, just as there are an infinite number of people, no two being exactly the same. Rewards will differ, Paul said, "as one star differeth from another." (1 Cor. 15:40-42)

While the hereafter will be a place of unimaginable peace and beauty, it is better described as a place of *eternal progress*, than a place of *eternal rest*. God, as the perfect Father, is concerned with our happiness, and as a being of perfect joy, He desires that we become more like Him. The concept that man, through positive experience and good choices, can become more like God is not a blasphemous "lessening" of God but a faithful "lifting" of man; and it is another gift of the restoration.

Gift 4: Enhanced Faith in God and in the Fairness of His Justice

A favored theme of professed atheists is that the injustice and random unfairness of life causes them to decline belief in God. They also often say that the traditional Christian concept of Heaven and Hell robs justice by being binary and arbitrary, and by its inherent assumption that a person born into Christendom can be saved while one born in a culture where Christ is unknown may be damned due to his unchosen ignorance.

Belief in a premortal existence and in a pre-judgment spirit world afterlife allows us also to believe and have faith in the perfect and eternal justice of God.

Life, to our limited and veiled mortal vision may look arbitrary and unfair. The obvious inequality of birth and opportunity sometimes seems to suggest uncaring randomness or even cruelty. Yet, when we expand and modify our vision with the belief in a pre-existence and in a loving and personal Heavenly Father, we can have faith that from His perspective what may seem random to us is both fair and purposeful. Apparent tragic circumstances may be unique chances for growth and for opportunities which are precisely what certain people need in the context of eternity.

And faith in an "equalizing" *spirit world* hereafter, where missed opportunities are made up, completes the logic of faith in a God who is ultimately fair, who loves *each* of His children as well as all of them, and who stands ready to help us in our needs but stops short of manipulating our lives without our request, thus preserving the *agency* which is essential to mortality's purpose.

God does not *create* fairness by seeing that our lives are equal or predictable or well-managed. Rather, He *insures* fairness by providing everyone, either on earth or in the spirit world, with an equal opportunity to accept Him and His Gospel.

To someone who walks into a track stadium and witnesses a race already in progress, the race may appear unfair. Some runners are ahead of others. The observer must see both the start and the finish of the race — and perhaps even the training that preceded it — before he will understand the cause-and-effect circumstances and realize that the race is fair.

The story is told of an Australian aborigine who "went walk-about" for over a year. During his absence, medical missionaries came to his tribe. By coincidence, on the very day he returned, his wife was undergoing an emergency appendectomy. He arrived just in time to see a white man cutting his wife open with a knife. To the aborigine, three conclusions were inescapable: 1. The man was trying to kill his wife, 2. It was being done against her will, 3. There was no chance of good coming of it.

All of the aborigine's conclusions were wrong, just as our conclusions are wrong if we judge from our short-sighted and limited perspective that God is cruel, arbitrary, unfair, or unjust.

A specific apostate doctrine that undermines the justice of God in the minds of men is the mainstream definition of "original sin" and its application to all of us. The term — *original sin* — itself is unfortunate. Adam did choose mortality and bring decay and death into the world but he did so not out of ignorance or folly; he did so as part of God's plan which *required* mortality and death.

We do all die because of Adam's act, but as Paul so clearly states, we will all be made alive because of Christ's act (1 Cor 15:21-23). Men are not punished for Adam's actions — rather, we forfeit rewards and progression by our own transgressions.

This knowledge, this reassurance, both of the fairness and justice of God and of the perfection of His plan, is a great gift of the restoration. The gift is more completely understood in connection with gift 5 which involves the *mercy* of God.

Once, during a vacation, we met an interesting couple who had left Christianity and embraced Hinduism. This seemed so rare and unlikely to me that I was bold enough to ask *why*.

"Well, basically," came the answer, "we felt the need for belief in a God who was *just*. As Christians we had trouble with the idea of original sin where we were all being pun-ished for Adam's sin. Also, we had no explanation for the random unfairness and inequality of human life on this earth. In Hinduism there is no original sin, and the concept of rein-carnation contains justice, because, over the course of many lives, our opportunities and blessings as well as our trials and sufferings will equal out."

I asked our new friends if they were aware that there was a Christian church — deeply and conservatively Christian — that viewed Adam differently (as the hero — the instigator of God's plan of agency) and that believed in the eternal, on-going nature of the spirit, moving not through different identities but through different realms which created a cumulative equality.

I now express this belief to you, Graham — the belief in a two-way eternity, in the perfect justice and perfect plan of God for our progress and growth, and in the fact that the promise of all this was another gift of the restoration.

Gift 5: A More Complete Comprehension of Christ, of His Atonement, and of Our Relationship to Him

All plans of agency and growth involve risk, and there is no true freedom without the opportunity to fail. This risk and this freedom are inherent in God's plan.

But without a mediator and a redeemer, the plan would have contained more than risk — it would have contained predictable and guaranteed universal failure. God has said that no unclean thing can enter His presence. He lives in a realm of perfection. Thus our bad choices, our human tendencies toward selfishness or laziness, and even the small inevitable mistakes of everyday life would, by definition, keep us from returning to Him.

Left to our own devices, the risks posed by this life are too great. The debts we accumulate to God, who gives us more than we can possibly repay, point us toward a debtor's prison rather than toward the palaces of the King. Sins, like tiny but tenacious barnacles, attach to our mortal hull and make us incapable of the slip speed and smooth perfection required to live with God.

And there is another barrier posed by mortality, one even more predictable than sin. It is that inevitable termination of temporal life which we call death. The very elements of time, change, deterioration, and "physicalness" that were set in motion by Adam's act (and that make mortality a test and growth-stage) also guarantee termination. We start dying the minute we are born.

God's goal for His children to become more like Him is not met by our mere sojourn in a brief and temporary physical existence. God Himself *has* a glorified, perfected body of flesh and bone, as witnessed by Biblical prophets and as intimated when He stated His intention to make man "in His image." God has (and is) both spirit and body and thus has the joy of (and the power over) both spiritual and physical matter and phenomenon. Our bodies are not the temporary apparatus of a brief physical experience in the earth-laboratory. They are prized, new possessions — joyful gifts from a loving Heavenly Father that have the potential to complete our *souls*. ("The spirit and the body are the soul of man.")

God's plan, therefore, required a means whereby physical death could be overcome and reversed and whereby the debt of sin could be relieved, repaid, and *redeemed*.

Only a sinless man with the unlimited credit of perfection could pay this debt and only a being who was the master rather than the subject of death could reverse the process of decay and deterioration, replacing it with regeneration and resurrection.

Jehovah, the first-born spirit Son of God and the pre-existent advocate of God's plan of mortality and agency, *gave* himself to this role.

He was the God of the Old Testament, of Moses and Abraham, and then He came to earth as Jesus Christ, Son of His mortal mother, Mary, and of His immortal father, God. He lived a life of utter perfection and taught a revolutionary new way of living and an outlook that centered on love and mercy. He presented the gospel of "good news," of hope and joy, and He died a voluntary death that paid for sin, fulfilled justice, and reversed and rolled back the momentum of the grave.

Few have taught the principles of Christ's ransom, sacrifice, and redemption better than your great country-man, C. S. Lewis. In his remarkable children's tale *The Lion, The Witch and The Wardrobe* he titles one chapter

"Deep Magic From The Dawn Of Time." In this chapter, the great lion Aslan (the Christ figure) offers himself in place of the boy who has committed treason and has thus become the claim of the White Witch (the Satan figure). Because of eternal justice, the witch "owns" the guilty boy, but justice is satisfied by Aslan's sacrifice as he gives his life to save the boy's. The witch laughs as she kills the Great Lion, believing that she has won.

But the next chapter is entitled "Deeper Magic From Before The Dawn of Time." In it, Aslan takes up his life again, having satisfied justice with mercy and having power over death through his perfection. Lewis doesn't try to explain *how* the deeper magic works — only to inspire awe in the fact that it does work.

The redemption and atonement of Jesus Christ, through our limited mortal minds, can be only partially and meta-phorically understood. The power and principles involved, the effort and suffering required, and the sheer magnitude of the consequences of His great sacrifice are all beyond our capacity to fully comprehend. Sometimes children, void of pretentious language and relying on faith and feeling more than on rational reason, handle this magnificent mystery best. When asking my six-year-old why Jesus came to earth, she responded with a single sentence: "To teach us to be nice and to show us how it will work when we die."

The resurrection is how it will work when we die. It will work for all mankind everywhere. As Paul said, "As in (because of) Adam, *all* die, even so in Christ shall *all* be made alive." All will be resurrected. It is part of God's plan that His children continue their progression with the com-pleted soul of spirit and body. Our resurrected bodies will be perfect and eternal, no longer subject to disease or deterioration. Where we will go with those bodies will depend on the lives we have lived, both here and in the pre-resurrection Spirit World) and on the outcome of the "self-judgment" mentioned earlier.

Christ will return to the earth and reign for one thousand years, during which time the work of salvation will be carried forth, partially through vicarious ordinances performed for those who died without opportunities to know of His plan. After all have had full and equal opportunities to accept Him, He will be our judge — merciful, perfectly empathetic, aware of our every pain and every desire. He will judge with the same mercy with which He lived and will reign forever in the Celestial Kingdom where His Father and those who have accepted His Father's plan will dwell.

It is important to understand that Christ's atonement overcame two *kinds* of death, both involving a separation. Physical death is the separation of the spirit and the body. It was instigated — for all mankind — by Adam. It has been overcome — for all mankind — by Christ. God's plan of agency, growth and self-choice, could be facilitated only by a descent into the suffering– and–ecstasy mix of mortality and the re-emergence into immortality.

The second kind of death is spiritual death which means the separation of man from God. It is brought on by our own transgressions. Christ atoned for our sins but our own repentance is what activates and puts into effect His forgiveness, allowing a return to God.

Salvation — the overcoming of physical death — is a free gift to all, but exaltation — the return to the presence of God, which is made possible by Christ's gift — must be earned.

With this deeper understanding of Christ's atonement comes a greater grasp of His majesty, and a more complete view of the *roles* that He plays in His Father's plan and in our personal and individual salvation. Let me illustrate this with a chart that compares ascending views of Christ — and points out the added levels or *dimensions* that the restoration has revealed about Him.

Twelve Levels of Belief in Christ

Level one: He did not exist. He is a myth.

Level two: He existed, but was only a trickster, a magician, a deceiver.

Level Three: He was a historical figure, but most of what is said about him is fiction or legend rather than history.

Level four: He was a remarkable and powerful teacher.

Level five: He was a charismatic leader and teacher who developed the most beautiful philosophy of life ever devised.

Level six: He was a prophet.

Level seven: He was the greatest of all the prophets.

Level eight: He was more than a man, more than a prophet — he was the Son of God.

Level nine: He was the Son of God and is our Savior. He died and atoned for our sins and was then resurrected.

Level ten: He was the Son of God and is our Savior. He established His church to preserve and spread His gospel.

Level eleven: He is the Son of God and is our Savior.
He established His church, but because
He had given man free agency He knew
that His church would be diluted and
destroyed. Following this apostasy and
following the "way- preparing" reformation, He has restored His complete
church and complete gospel back to
earth.

Level twelve: The divine Savior has restored his
church. Through his full gospel, we
know him as the Firstborn, the Creator,
the God of the Old Testament, the Only
Begotten, the Atoning One, the just God
who visited and taught in both hemi-
spheres and in the spirit world, the
Restorer, the Head of his church today,
our Eternal Elder Brother, our Judge.

True Christians emerge at levels eight and nine, and
believers in the restoration at levels eleven and twelve. Let
me now add one more chart or table, Graham, which lists
the *roles* played by Jesus Christ in God's plan of salvation.
Note that many of them are partially understood through
The Bible but enhanced and expanded as a further gift of the
restoration.

The "Roles" of Jesus Christ

1. A great intelligence prior to his (and our) spiritual
    creation.
2. The firstborn spirit son of our Heavenly Father.
3. A great and loyal leader in the spirit world.

4. The leading advocate of the plan of agency and redemption for this mortal existence, and the one who insisted that all credit and glory be given to the Father.

5. The accepted volunteer for the supremely difficult and self-sacrificing implementation of that plan of agency and redemption.

6. The creator of the world.

7. The light of the world.

8. Jehovah, the God of the Old Testament.

9. The Only begotten Son of the Father in the flesh.

10. The only perfect man ever to live.

11. The head of the original Church of Jesus Christ.

12. The teacher of the full gospel ("good news").

13. The Savior and Redeemer of the world who willingly gave His life for us all.

14. The first fruits of a glorious resurrection, which, because of Him, will apply to us all.

15. The direct, resurrected teacher of the gospel to His "other sheep" — in the spirit world, in the Americas,* to the lost ten tribes.

16. The Mediator with the Father.

17. The restorer of the fullness of His Gospel.

18. The Lord who will come again and reign during the Millennium.

19. Our judge.

20. Our father, if we accept Him and live His commandments.

What greater gift could there be than a deeper, fuller, more complete understanding of our Lord and Savior, Jesus Christ?

---

*More on this in Gift 12.

Gift 6: The Gift of the Holy Ghost

When we speak of gifts, the term is nowhere better applied (and nowhere more *scripturally* applied) than to the *gift* of the Holy Ghost. The New Testament clearly states that the apostles of Jesus and other holders of His priesthood power gave this gift by the laying on of hands . . . by placing their hands on the heads of those who had repented and been baptized and literally bestowing upon them the companionship and the guidance of the Holy Spirit.

The Holy Ghost is the third member of the Godhead. Just as Christ is a separate being from (and the son of) God the Father, so is the Holy Ghost a separate and distinct individual. The three are one* in purpose, perfectly united in the object of mankind's progress and salvation, but they are three distinct and individual beings.

Even as the roles of Creator, Savior and Judge are played by Jesus Christ, acting under the direction and for the glory of God, His Father — so are the essential roles of Testifier, Comforter, and Spirit of Truth played by the Holy Ghost.

Unlike the Father and the Son, both of whom have perfected, tangible bodies, the Holy Ghost is, for now, a personage of spirit. As such He has the God-given power and charge to bear witness of truth to our spirits.

By the power of the Holy Ghost we may "know the truth of all things." Through this power and gift we have access to the feelings and impressions that allow us to separate truth and error, that guide us toward our truest

---

*The confusing doctrine of "trinity" that resulted from the compromises and reconciliations of the Nicene and Athanasian councils in the early Christian centuries put the term "one" completely out of context. The meaning of the term is clear in the seventeenth chapter of John where Christ, praying to His Father, (not praying to Himself) asks that His apostles might become one "As we are one."

destinies, and that enhance our understanding of the world we live in and of our individual place in that world.

This spirit of truth and insight is available to all men everywhere. It is the reason why sincere and seeking minds, even when they exist in circumstances void of books or contact with earthly *sources* of knowledge, nonetheless gather understanding and *arrive* at truth. The Holy Ghost can accurately be called a Conscience, a Revealer, a Comforter, and a Spirit of Truth. Indeed, the scriptures *do* call Him these things. His influence penetrates the veil of forgetfulness to the extent that we sense or feel some of the realities about ourselves and about God that are veiled from our conscious memory. This is why, as we discover spiritual truth, we often have the feeling that we are *remembering* or *re-learning* rather than finding for the first time.

While all honest seekers (particularly those who pray) can feel and benefit from this spirit, the true and complete *gift* of the Holy Ghost is given today as it was anciently — by the laying on of hands by those holding God's priesthood *to* those who have been baptized and thus prepared by the remission of their sins for the companionship of the Holy Ghost.

Gift 7: The Gift of the Priesthood

Giving the gift of the Holy Ghost, the effectual perform-
ing of emersion baptism, and all other ordinances which by
physical symbol and prayer actually invoke and involve
God's power and bring about a spiritual change . . . all such
acts require the *Priesthood.* Priesthood, in the Biblical
sense, was God's authority, controlled by Prophets and
Apostles and given to worthy individuals by the laying on of
hands. Men did not assume this power, or purchase it, or
earn it by the completion of some course of study or aca-
demic degree (see John 15:16; Acts 8:18-20). Rather, it was
given by God, through His apostles, to those who had made
baptism covenants and who were worthy to wield God's
power.

It is so today. An integral part of the restored Gospel is
the restored Priesthood. Through its righteous use, sins are
washed away through baptism, the sick are healed, the gift
of the Holy Ghost is bestowed, Patriarchal blessings of
guidance and personal prophecy are given from one genera-
tion to the next, and ordinances are performed in holy
temples which unite families for eternity and bind men to
God through the exchange of sacred covenants and
promises.

Today, the restored Priesthood of God allows men to
act in the name of God and it is a powerful gift of the
restoration.

Gift 8: Eternal Marriages and Deeper Family Ties

Marriages that are performed in Mormon temples are not "till death do you part" but "for time and all eternity." Mortal life, as it affords us our first opportunity for parenthood and procreation, also marks the beginning of our own personal kingdoms or eternal families. The bonds of husband and wife in marriage and of parent and child in families are too deep and sacred, and too eternally important, to be voided at death. Instead, they endure and strengthen as we move on to further stages of our growth and progress.

Mormon family life, and the solidarity of marriages performed in temples is widely known, almost legendary. Graham, you have observed first hand the importance we place in our marriage and the priorities we and other Mormon families place on our relationships with each other. Some observers assume that this is brought about by the extensive programs, manuals, organized activities and other assistance provided by the Church for families. In fact, it is our *beliefs* that are the cause. Beliefs about the nature and purpose of families bring about strong families and it is those strong families that drive the Church's programs and efforts.

The beliefs that are the cause involve "both sides" of eternity. The belief in a pre-existence causes us to view our children not as tiny, beginning sprouts of life that our bodies have produced but as our brothers and sisters, belonging to and coming from our Heavenly Father, just as we did. Thus we respect them as siblings and care for them as our stewardships.

And the belief in the potential eternal nature of marriage and families causes us to think further ahead, to be more committed and to be convinced that no challenge is too great and no effort too much to ask when the endurance of our deepest love is at stake.

We do not think that we love our spouses, our children, or our parents more than other people might, but we believe there is a purpose, an insight, and a meaning in that love that could not be present without faith in what came before and in what goes after . . . a gift we would not have but through the restoration.

Personal Note:
A Gospel That Is Both Lyrical and Logical

Graham, before this begins to sound more like a book or a lecture than a letter, let me get back to the personal and to the day-to-day. I wrote parts of this letter over the last couple of days, after work, early in the morning, etc., hoping that it would take on a logical and practical tone. Then early this morning I drove up into a flaming, bright autumn canyon, looking for some peace and quiet and for the kind of inspiration that I hoped would help me focus and capture the rest of what I want to say to you. The day was breathtakingly beautiful . . . one of those rare, perfect autumn days with cloudless sky and brilliant, slanting sunlight in which the maples were bright pink and the aspen was burnished gold, set off by the deep evergreen of fir and pine. The oaks (you'll remember that we call them "scrub oak" since at this altitude they never become massive or strong like your great English oaks) were the brightest pure red I have ever seen. By the time I got to our little ranch, I had realized that it was too rare a day to go inside and write, so I saddled up our Appaloosa horse "Banner" and rode up into the hills.

I love alpine autumn scenery, I love to drive through fall foliage, but I've found that you don't see it *all* until you are on horseback. The rhythm of the hoofs and the effortless movement *through* the beauty somehow enhances everything. I was *moved*, awed by the beauty.

As I rode high up into the narrow canyon, beside a cascading stream, my mind went back to this letter and ideas started to come. I stopped periodically and made notes which I've since tried to incorporate and integrate. Let me try to express some of the feelings I had, thinking about you and what I wanted to say to you as I rode through the autumn mountains.

Feeling 1: As I rode, I realized that much of what I want to say to you sounds more lyrical than logical. And maybe that's why I want to say it. The wonder of the restored gospel is that it is both lyrical and logical, both sensitive and sensible, both pretty and profound. All real truth is also real beauty. (I think it was your poet Keats who said that.) We are never forced to choose between the mental and the emotional. When something is true and from God, our heart testifies of it to our mind and our mind testifies back to our heart. The teachings of the restored gospel have the *ring* of truth which energizes and excites both heart and mind.

Feeling 2: As I rode higher on the mountain path, a path I had never been on before, I was struck by the adventure of it all. I did not know what would be around the next bend, but I anticipated *more* beauty — possibly some danger and a risk or two, but I wanted to be there — I wanted to see it, to move on, to discover.

So much of life can be the same. We've never been exactly where we are until right now — and it's never been this late before, it's never been *now* before. One of the gifts of the restored gospel is that we can see mortality as an exciting and experience–filled adventure. God *gave* us all this beauty, all these options. The earth is an elaborate, orbiting laboratory where we can mix elements in ways that create an unending range of possibilities and results. We were sent here to *find* our deepest selves, and the world was designed and created to help us do so.

Feeling 3: A couple of times, there *were* rough spots and dangers around the next bend. In one place the stream bed was deceptively soft and Banner sunk in to his knees and had to kick and scramble to get out. I got off his back so I could lead him to higher, firmer ground. In another place the path was washed away on a steep hillside. I decided to take a detour and come back to the trail up ahead. Each time there was a feeling of satisfaction and fulfillment for having *surpassed* the danger — overcoming it and learning from it.

In life, it is the overcoming of difficulties, the solving of problems, the working out of dilemmas that brings real joy and growth. It's the accepting of (and sometimes the creation of) challenges that make life exciting. The scriptures tell us to "watch and pray" — to be aware in spirit and in mind, and thus to make right decisions that allow us to move through and beyond and into realms of *more* beauty.

Feeling 4: New metaphors seemed to multiply out of my ride. I would think of Banner, my horse, as he scrambled up a bank or jumped over a falling log. He is so powerful. I felt his strength, so superior to mine, as he gathered himself to climb, to run. Controlled, his power is such a joy.

On the way home, I let him run, and in his desire to get back to hay and barn, he tried to run away — too fast for a rocky trail. I reigned him in, *bridled* him hard to control the power that can so quickly turn from joy to danger.

Just as the spirit must bridle the body.

What a dark tragedy that so much of the world's religion *blames* the body, condemns it as the source of evil and the test and scourge of man, even urges us to kill our passions. I wouldn't kill my horse — for in him is power and joy and *capacity* which becomes mine. The body allows our control of and our enjoyment of physical things. In its appetites and powers lies danger but we have the reigns in our hands and, well-bridled, our physical bodies provide us potential to climb to heights of joy and of experience that we could otherwise never imagine.

Gift 9: The Gift of Gratitude, Confidence and Humility

Philosophers have so often equated gratitude with joy, and linked the capacity to be thankful, to be moved, to be awed with the capacity to feel deeply and truly happy.

Humility, too, is prerequisite to real happiness. No one has ever spoken of the importance of humility more eloquently (or more entertainingly) than another of your great Christian countrymen, G. K. Chesterton, who said, "If man would make his world large, he must make himself small . . . towers are not tall unless we look up at them; and giants are not giants unless they are larger than we . . . it is impossible without humility to enjoy anything, even pride." One gift of the restoration is the added capacity it gives us to feel both great gratitude and great humility.

Real gratitude needs both a subject and an object. We need someone to be grateful *to* as well as something to be grateful *for*. Knowing God as a personal father who has given us all we have and Christ as a supreme elder brother who has given the ultimate gift of redemption makes it possible to feel otherwise unobtainable levels of thankfulness, wonder, and awe.

Besides additional gratitude, worship of a personal and loving Heavenly Father can provide extra measures of confidence and humility. These two qualities, often thought of as opposites, come in their deepest sense *together*, and from the same source. Knowledge of God's greatness and of our smallness as His infant spirit children produces humility — yet an understanding that we *are* His children, with access to His heritage as well as to His help, provides the deepest kind of confidence.

Just as a man might gaze at the vast and starry night sky and ponder his own smallness and insignificance compared with the endless handiwork of God, so he might also feel the seeds of incredible importance and confidence as he reflects that he is not merely the handiwork but the actual *offspring* of God.

What a gift it is to have the enhanced gratitude and both the humility and the confidence that comes through knowing our relationship to our Heavenly Father.

Gift 10: The Gift of Potential and Promises

I wrote earlier of the divisive conflict in the premortal world where Lucifer's proposal of coercion and guarantee was pitted against Christ and the Father's plan of agency and self-determination. One could describe the division in more political terms by saying it was a debate between advocates of *enforced equality* and those of *equality of opportunity*. We who preferred the latter knew full well that our choice included the opportunity (or the risk) to fail; but we also knew, as God did, that without the ultimate downside, there could be no ultimate upside. The ultimate upside is nothing less than becoming as God is.

Perhaps of all the statements ever made by church leaders, the one that has fostered the most misunderstanding and criticism is Joseph Smith's couplet, "As man is, God once was; and as God is, man may become."

"Blasphemy," outsiders have screamed, accusing the church of lessening the role and stature of God.

On the contrary! As mentioned earlier, the concept merely elevates the potential of man; and it can be grasped only in the *eternal* context where the vastness of the gap between God and man is approachable because of the endless timetable on which we have to work. The statement does not lessen the distance between God's perfection and our uncountable imperfections. It simply *defines* the difference as one of *degree* rather than one of *kind*.

The gift of knowledge of limitless potential assures us not only of the powers within us, but of the total love of our Heavenly Father. A loving Father cannot help but want His children to gain the joy and the good that He has gained. God has gained all joy and all good and His work and His glory is to bring about our eternal life and immortal joy.

The desire of God for His children to progress and gradually become more like Him is perhaps the mind and spirit's most logical thought. Emerson spoke of this earth as a "God factory" where men learn lessons that shorten the distance between what they are and what God is. More currently, best-selling psychiatrist-author, Scott Peck, in his book *The Road Less Traveled* (which continues to ride the best-seller lists more than twenty-five years after its first publication) concludes that "all of us who postulate a loving God come to a single terrifying idea — God wants us to become Himself. We are growing toward Godhood."*

Nothing is more exciting than potential. Nothing is more terrifying and more awesome than ultimate potential.

Knowing not only of God's love for us but of His plan for our progress and of the two-way eternity in which we exist, makes the process of growth one of *discovery* as well as one of *becoming*. We already *are* so much, because of our eternity of growth as His children. We each have gifts and talents and aptitudes that are unique among all human-kind. We are rare and unique not only by virtue of genetics and environment, but by virtue of the legacy and develop-ment of our premortal lives. In mortality we have the physical tools and experience necessary to discover more deeply who we *have* become as well as to decide what we *will* become.

We are not pre-destined to anything because our agency is real. But we are "fore-ordained," by our prior develop-ment and by God's individual hopes and wishes for each of us, to make certain contributions, to do certain things here on this earth that no one else could do, to find the right mountain for ourselves, and to climb it. This challenge, along with God's promise that we can return to His presence, is another gift of the restoration.

---

*M. Scott Peck, *The Road Less Traveled*. New York, NY: Simon & Schuster, 1970, p. 269.

Gift 11: The Gift of Purpose, Priorities, Programs and Practical Guidelines

Once during our first stay in England (while I was a mission president), I had an interesting discussion with an elderly Englishman who lived across the street from our Mormon chapel in Southampton. I had come early to prepare for a speech that I would make there that evening, and as I pulled up in front of the church, this man was digging in his front garden. I said hello and we began a friendly chat.

After a moment he said, "Well, listen, since you go to this church, maybe you can answer a question I've had for years. What goes on in there all week? The lights are always on! Pleasant, well-behaved people of all ages seem to be in and out every evening and sometimes during the day! Are they the same people that come on Sunday? What happens in there the rest of the week?"

It turned into a long discussion. I explained to him that our religion wasn't just for Sunday, that it was a whole way of life, that it dealt with the physical and the social as well as with the spiritual, that our churches included cultural halls with stages and basketball courts as well as chapels and classrooms, that there were youth activities, women's and men's auxiliaries, children's meetings, scouting, athletic events, dances, charitable drives, and all manner of active programs.

I sincerely invited him to cross the street and drop in to see for himself whenever the lights were on.

Graham, it is important to know that besides the doctrines, teachings, and insights of what we call the Restored Gospel, there is the gift of the Church itself — the organization and programs and practical guides of the institution that I mentioned briefly in an earlier letter.

It has always been so in the Lord's church. Christ set up an actual church organization that included Apostles, Priests, Pastors, Deacons, Teachers, etc.* who were to exercise control of the priesthood power and to establish the practical people-helping programs of the Church. Paul admonished the early saints to "meet together oft" and to teach and learn from each other. The officials and leaders in Christ's church were lay people — none was paid and all had other livelihoods as is the case in the Church today.

Virtually every active member has a "church job" which may be Bishop of a congregation, or class teacher, or chorister, or nursery leader, or clerk, or chairman of the Christmas social.

Members are visited in their homes once a month by "home teachers" who look out for the economic and temporal well-being of those they visit as well as giving spiritual support. The Church's famous "welfare program" gives everyone a chance to work voluntarily in local church-owned factories or farms and anyone who is unemployed or without adequate income can work more than his share and earn the sustenance he needs.

The church's missionary system, about which you know so much, currently involves more than fifty thousand full-time young men and women who serve voluntarily at their own or their family's expense in virtually every corner of the world. They perform humanitarian service as well as sharing their beliefs, and they return after two years more mature, more culturally aware, often with a second language and always more clear on what they want to do professionally, and more prepared to live productive lives.

---

*Ephesians 4:11-14.

The real measurement of the church's effect in the lives of its members can best be measured not by the number of programs or activities, but by the countenances and faces of its members — in their outlooks on life and the happiness and solidarity of their families.

You, who have spoken so eloquently on the "fruits" of the Mormon Church, do not need to be reminded of any of these things. I bring them up only as a preface to Christ's statement, "By their fruits ye shall know them."

The Church's teachings are eminently practical and timely in any era. The "Word of Wisdom" health code warned against the use of alcohol, tobacco, and caffeine long before their harmful effects were discovered medically. The ancient (and current) practice of the tithe teaches discipline and keeps the Church financially solvent and finances its continuing dramatic growth. (On average, two new churches are finished and dedicated somewhere in the world every day.)

The practical day-to-day *results* of the Church's influence in the lives of its members is best summarized in the Church's 13th "Article of Faith" penned by Joseph Smith:

> "We believe in being honest, true, chaste,
> benevolent, virtuous, and in doing good to all men. .
> . . If there is anything virtuous, lovely, or of good
> report, or praiseworthy, we seek after these things."

Gift 12: The Gift of Continuity and Consistency

In a world where the only constant is change, how much we need and want continuity and consistency. Since these are so hard to find in man's mortality, we must look for them in God's eternity . . . in our religion and in our faith.

Sadly, most of the world's religious history is a study in inconsistency and broken continuity. While religious causes advocate peace, they have been the principal precipitator of many of the world's greatest wars. While they preach unity, they often create polarization and division. And while they teach of prophets and direct manifestations from God to man in ancient days, they deny the continuation or existence of either today.

With the restoration of The Church of Jesus Christ came the reassuring gift of God's consistency and continuity, His renewed promise that He is "the same yesterday, today, and forever." At least six important *kinds* of continuity are manifest and revealed through the restoration.

A. *The continuity of man and of his individual progress.* The knowledge that we lived before and will continue to live after this life gives us faith that nothing is wasted, that all we do and experience has a long-range and ultimate purpose.

B. *The continuity of God's dealings with man.* Some who speculate that God no longer communicates with man today as He did with His ancient prophets have tried to guess at *why*. Three possible reasons exist: (1) God has lost the power to speak to man. (2) God does not care for us as much as He did for ancient people and so He chooses not to speak. (3) We don't need His voice any more — we have progressed past that need.

The first reason is blasphemous, the second insulting to ourselves and to God, and the third absurd.

God does still speak to prophets, and they are no more obscure or hard to find today than in earlier times. All we need is the faith to seek and to hear. What the Old Testament prophet Amos said is still true. "Surely the Lord God will do nothing but He revealeth His secret to His servants the prophets." (Amos 3:7)

Even the pattern of apostasy and restoration is a testimony to God's continuity. Biblical scripture records six separate "dispensations" or "restorations" of truth — each of the last five following a time of apostasy and confusion that left the world void of cohesive truth. Such apostasies and "strayings" are a natural consequence of the plan of agency and self-determination that God has committed himself to in our behalf.

Enoch, Noah, Abraham and Moses were all prophets of restoration — prophets through which God restored truth that had originally existed in Adam's first dispensation, but had been lost in the confusion and compromise (and wickedness) that preceded each of the prophets' lives. In the sixth dispensation, Christ himself brought His gospel to the earth and performed the atonement so that all men both before and after could be saved.

But the pattern continued. Few serious students of history would deny the apostasy that began in the second century and spread through the Dark Ages, leaving Christianity splintered, diluted, and ritualized.[*]

The reformation that occurred in the 16th, 17th and 18th centuries, and the restoration that happened in the 19th century were a continuation of the pattern and a further testament of the continuity of God and of His purposes and patterns.

---

[*]See appendix for further comment on the apostasy.

C. *The continuity of scripture.* At the end of the *Book of Revelation,* on the last page of the *Holy Bible,* we find a warning against "adding anything to this book." Some have taken this phrase as a signal that the cannon of scripture was complete, that no more would be either revealed or written.

Yet this cannot be the case for several reasons: 1. When this phrase was written, *The Bible* did not exist as a compiled book; 2. Other books in *The Bible,* even early books in the Old Testament, carry the same warning, obviously meaning not to add to or alter that particular book within scripture; 3. There *were* other books of scripture that did not survive for inclusion in the King James compilation which of course came together more than a thousand years following John's writing of Revelations; 4. Because it is both illogical and inconsistent (and God is neither) to suddenly seal the Heavens; and 5. *The Bible* is the history and sacred writ of only one group of people and God is the God of all people.

The canon of scripture has always been dynamic, never static. God's word and direction, when given to man and recorded, *is* scripture.

The natural process of restoration that began in 1820 included the restoration of lost scripture.

Christ, who said clearly that He had come to the Jews and the House of Israel and that others would take His message to the Gentiles, *also* said clearly that He had "other sheep" (other members of the House of Israel) who were "not of this fold. Them also must I bring."*

One gift of the restoration and a testament of God's continuity is a second scriptural witness of Jesus Christ called *The Book of Mormon.* As part of the restoration, God revealed this hidden record which contained the religious

---

*John 10:14-16.

and secular history of a group of Israelites who left
Jerusalem just before the Babylonian captivity of 600 B.C.
and settled the American continents. The record supports
The Bible in remarkable ways and records the visit of Jesus
Christ to the Americas following His resurrection. In every
way, the book is a gift — a gift of faith, a gift of additional
witness, a gift of powerful and compelling history, and a gift
of deep insight and spiritual perception.

D. *The continuity of Individual Inspiration and Recognition of Truth*

God has always rewarded the faith of sincere inquiry
with promptings, feelings, and answers through his spirit.
His continuity in this pattern is beautifully reiterated in the
promise He makes in the restored *Book of Mormon* scripture. Near the conclusion of this second scriptural witness
of Christ and His gospel, these words appear: ". . . And
when ye shall receive these things, I would exhort you that
ye would ask God, the eternal Father, if these things are not
true. And if ye shall ask with a sincere heart, with real
intent, having faith in Christ, He will manifest the truth of it
unto you by the power of the Holy Ghost."

I know you understand, Graham, that the purpose of
this letter is not to try to debate or to convert you through
logic or reason of the truth of the restoration. People do
not, as we have often discussed, discover or gain conviction
of spiritual truths through mental processes of deduction
and analysis. Spiritual knowledge comes through the witness of the spirit, as *The Book of Mormon* scripture above
so clearly points out. The only hope a person should have in
telling another person about his personal spiritual convictions, is that the other person will be touched or impressed
to the point that he will, through prayer, seek his own
spiritual answer.

E. *Continuity in the organization of the Church.* The officers and offices of Christ's original Church were charged with "the perfecting of the saints, the work of the ministry and the edifying of the body of Christ."* The apostles controlled the Priesthood and authorized its succession. The other officers each filled specific roles and performed certain duties, like links in a chain. But, as I mentioned earlier, persecution divided the early apostles and cut them off from each other, and they were unable to fill vacancies as they had done before (when an apostle died, the other eleven met in fasting and prayer and God, through them, chose a successor — see Acts I). As the apostles were martyred, a critical link in the chain was dissolved and the true Priesthood dwindled and died. Without its leadership and God's guidance through its channel, plain and precious teachings were lost — churches in different locations began to diverge on doctrines, and truth-diluting compromises resulted.

It was the breakdown and destruction of the Church's structure and organization that precipitated the loss and changing of Christ's teachings.

In restoring His Church, Christ restored continuity by re-instituting the organization of His Church. All officers in the Church today, from the twelve apostles on down are identical to those in His original Church. The Church, now as then, bears His name. The Church of Jesus Christ of Latter-Day Saints is identical — in fact is the same as — in fact is *one* with The Church of Jesus Christ of Former-Day Saints.**

---

*Ephesians 4:12.
**"Saint" in the New Testament was designation for all church members. Paul wrote to the saints of Ephesis, etc.

F. *Continuity of the gifts of the spirit.* We believe in prophecy, revelation, visions, healing, etc. We believe in miracles! Supernatural occurrences are not contrary to natural law — they are concurrent and in harmony with higher laws of God which are triggered by our righteousness and faith.

As you have often said, Graham, God's plan includes perfect and intricate "spiritual circuitry" into which man can "plug" if he finds the correct frequency of humility and faith.

Within our physical bodies, we are spiritual beings, and our spirits have the capacity to communicate (both "sending" and "receiving") with God's spirit. The feelings of the spirit are the surest source of knowledge, far more trustworthy than sight or sound.

I'm reminded of a powerful example of spiritual receptivity that happened in that same Southampton chapel (where the lights are always on). As the "mission president," I had driven down from our mission headquarters in Surrey to meet with a group of our young missionaries during the day and to then speak at an evening meeting. There was an hour or two between the meetings and it was a lovely autumn day, so I took a drive around the city. On a small residential street, I happened past a road-side display of homemade baskets and noticed a blind man standing by with his dog. I stopped to look and learned that the man's name was George and that he was both the maker and the seller of the baskets. As we chatted, it became clear that George was a man of humor and of pride. I asked if he made all the baskets. He replied, "All but the dog baskets — the dog made those."

He told me he had been blind for 30 years, but quickly added, "Don't pity me. You have one sense that is better than mine, but I have four that are better than yours. I can hear, taste, feel and smell better than you can."

I bought a basket and we talked for some time. As I left, I asked if I could send some missionaries to talk with him about Christ. He said yes.

A month later, I had another speech scheduled in Southampton. When I arrived, the missionary leader announced that instead of the regular meeting there would be a baptism, "And President," he said, "if it's all right with you, we would like you to perform the baptism."

Puzzled but agreeing, I went to the dressing room to don white clothing (baptisms are performed by total emersion according to Christ's pattern and by the authority of His restored Priesthood). I opened the door to the dressing room and there was George, already dressed in white. He knew who I was before I spoke, and we embraced. "Tell me the story of your conversion, George," I asked. He said it was a simple story. The missionaries had visited him — he had again felt the calm, sure spirit that he said he felt when he and I met. The next Sunday he had attended church. "Remember I told you I could *feel* more clearly and deeply than sighted people? Well, when I walked into this church, I felt truth and light, and I knew I had found Christ's Church."

The spirit *is* real. And the feelings it prompts within us are the surest witness of truth that we can have. The gifts of the spirit and the powers of Priesthood and of faith are also real. Miracles are performed by these powers every day.

You were part of one miracle in our lives, Graham. Remember when I rushed Linda to the tiny Epsom hospital with serious hemorrhaging ten weeks before the due date of our son? I gave her a Priesthood blessing and felt the assurance that all would be well. Then I felt prompted to call you and ask who was the best obstetrician in London. You told me of Dr. Gordon. I called him from the lobby of the hospital and he broke all records driving his big white Jaguar from London out to Epsom where he relieved the struggling young Pakistani intern who to that point was the only doctor caring for Linda. He managed to stop the hemorrhaging and then got in his car and headed back toward London. He had been gone for scarcely ten minutes when Linda's bleeding started again — even more severely. With the fear of inexperience in his eyes, the young intern announced in broken English that he was going to have to perform an emergency Caesarian. I walked out to a grove of trees and prayed as I perhaps had never prayed before. I looked up to see the white Jaguar screeching around the corner and back into the car park. I ran and opened Dr. Gordon's car door as he came to a stop, yelling that Linda was on her way to surgery. With a quick nod he was off, going up the hospital steps two at a time, pulling off his coat as he ran. I returned to the trees to pray.

Later a nurse told me she had been in obstetrics for 20 years and had never seen a more masterful or *fast* Caesarian. She told me that anything slower would have cost the baby's life — and perhaps Linda's. She said that she and the other nurses now called the doctor, "Flash Gordon."

Still later I asked Dr. Gordon why he came back, and he shook his head and said, "It was just a feeling."

Two days later, I again used the Priesthood, this time to bless that tiny infant who had stopped breathing, my hands thrust through the holes in the incubator. As you know, that baby is now our biggest boy, a strapping, healthy six-foot-six teenager.

The power of God and the gifts of the spirit are real, more real in fact, than anything else. I know that you know that also, Graham. Gifts of the spirit are open and available to all who pursue them. They are a part of reality for all who sense that there is something higher and deeper and more lasting than this life. One of the gifts of the restoration is that we can understand these spiritual forces more clearly and know more personally the Source from which they come . . . and we know of the continuity and constancy of that Force throughout all the ages of time.

The Wrappings

In an attempt to help some young students appreciate the intricacies and perfect utility of nature, I once gave a class the challenge of designing the perfect snack food. It had to be sweet and tasty, it had to be nourishing and healthful, it had to keep well, and it had to have the perfect packaging or wrapping. After all kinds of suggestions of perfect candy bars, gum balls and cupcakes, someone finally gave me the answer I wanted — an *apple*.

Some still argued for the taste of candy or the nutrition of a granola bar, but no one would argue against the apple's packaging. It was beautiful. It preserved the apple, and it was *edible*.

Now that we have talked about twelve of the gifts of the restoration, let's talk about the wrappings. Before the gifts are understood, before their magnitude is appreciated, the wrappings may seem bright and overwhelming to the point of distraction. They may seem out of place in our world of the natural day-to-day — because the wrappings are supernatural. Man can no more fathom their makeup than he can manufacture an apple skin.

The wrappings of the gifts of the restoration are the *process* of restoration. They include golden plates on which ancient scripture was engraved, visitations from angelic messengers to a boy prophet, and yes, an earthly appearance of our Eternal Father and of His Son, our Savior, Jesus Christ.

Magnificent wrappings! Spectacular and supernatural so far beyond our usual frame of reference that they seem unreal. *But they are the most real thing we know!* And, having considered the gifts, how could they appropriately be wrapped in anything less.

The wrappings, when they are understood, are gifts in and of themselves. They are as edible and as nourishing as the gifts they contain. They are the gifts of continuing revelation and the continuing "openness" of the Heavens. They are, like Gift 12, a gift of continuity — an assurance that God still loves and reveals truth to His children.

God and Christ, consistent in their pattern of restoring lost truth when the world contains sufficient truth seekers, came to the gifted and seeking young man, Joseph Smith, who became the first prophet of a new dispensation. That first visitation was a gift, restoring the knowledge that God and Christ are separate beings with oneness of purpose, restoring the understanding that God is a being of form — of flesh and bone, and that we are literally made in His image, literally His children, and restoring the assurance that God loves all men of all ages.

Following the first vision, the restoration unfolded in an orderly and beautifully logical way. Doctrine was restored and confusion swept aside by the gift of new scripture (actually very old scripture, brought forth anew by the miraculous translation of *The Book of Mormon* — America's ancient, Christ- witnessing history — from the thin sheets of gold on which the ancients wrote it). The book became a second witness of Christ, strengthening and supplementing *The Bible* — clear and specific in some areas of doctrine where *The Bible* is general and vague.

The restoration of the Priesthood and apostolic power came in equally logical ways. John the Baptist, the very being who baptized the Savior, returned to earth as an angelic messenger and conferred the Aaronic Priesthood by the laying on of hands. Peter, James, and John, the Lord's three chief apostles in His original church, returned to restore the higher Melchizedek Priesthood and the apostleship which controlled the Priesthood and authorized its offices and succession.

The wrappings, in order to be complete, had to surround and protect all of the gifts. The process of restoration, to be complete, had to reveal and reconstitute all of the original teachings, ordinances, and organization of Jesus' church. Doctrines and insights that were not fully clear even in the combined scripture of *The Bible* and *The Book of Mormon* were restored directly to Joseph Smith in visions and answers to prayer. They became sections of a third volume of scripture called *The Doctrine and Covenants* and include such things as a fuller explanation of the hereafter and of the purpose (and process) of eternal marriage and families.

As the gifts of the restoration are contemplated, it becomes ever more clear that no other wrappings — no other process of restoration would do.

And the process is *ongoing*. Living apostles continue on the earth. We are led by a living prophet today. As the world changes and our own personal challenges and temptations alter with the times, God continues to give both individual guidance through personal inspiration and collective guidance through His prophet.

Preceded by faith and repentance, the ordinance of baptism is the entry . . . taking us inside the protection, beauty, and knowledge of the wrappings, letting us partake both of them and of the gifts inside — the gifts of the social, emotional, and spiritual blessings of the church and the gifts of insight and comprehension.

To assist us in our insight, baptized church members are given The Gift of the Holy Ghost by the laying on of hands. Now, as in ancient times, this gift stretches the veil and opens our souls to the spiritual side of life.

The Cost of the Gifts

(what one gives up for them)

Graham, when I think of you, I am filled with an admiration, a respect, and a friendship that I feel for few people. Linda joins me in these feelings. You have achieved the highest honors of men — all well deserved. More importantly, you continue to live a life of energy, excitement, and commitment. You are a valiant man, Graham, as well as a virtuous one. There is no doubt that you will continue to excel, continue to contribute. Any connotations of retirement or rest that the honors of senior statesmanship usually imply will be entirely lost on you.

As interested and as involved as you are in the state of the world, I know that you are even more interested in the one question that is larger — namely the state of the soul.

This letter and the previous discussions we have had are only beginnings. The pursuit of "testimony" or of personal conviction and knowledge of these things is an arduous one, but its only requirements are sincerity, real intent, faith, energy and the desire for truth — qualities that you have in abundance; surpassing, I believe, anyone else that I know.

Are there *costs* in addition to requirements? Things that must be *given up* in order to accept the gifts? There are — and the costs are different for different people. Some have to change their personal habits and entire life styles and reverse their world-views. Such would not be the case for you.

As a great helper and defender of the church, you have already paid some costs. There have been those, I'm sure, who question your assistance and friendship to an institution of such minority position and such frequent misunderstanding. As you accept more of the gifts, these peer questions would come with more volume and more frequency. In embracing all of the gifts, you would become (despite the vast English roots of the church) the first member of the British political establishment ever to do so.

So there are costs, despite the fact that the gifts are freely given. But the main requirement is asking God for sure answers about the truth of the gifts. With the answers will come both the motivation and the strength for implementation.

In the third book of scripture spoken of earlier, there is a verse that says:

> "For what doth it profit a man if a gift is bestowed upon him, and he receive not the gift? Behold, he rejoices not in that which is given unto him, neither rejoices in him who is the giver of the gift."

God is the giver of the gift, Graham. You and I are both partakers. You have already received enough (and *given* enough) to assure that you and I will always rejoice in our friendship — a friendship which I feel, even as I write, will continue to deepen despite distance and which will return to us each even more than we invest.

All the best,
Richard M. Eyre

APPENDIX

Some years ago, I was contacted by a publisher who planned to publish a book comparing the views of various religions on the subject of life after death.

Would I, he inquired, write the chapter on the Mormon or Latter-day Saint version of after-life? I explained that I was not an official or general officer of the Church and that I could only respond personally, not officially. He indicated that he understood that the Church was a lay church and that what he wanted was a response from a lay member. I then indicated that I felt the church's views on the afterlife could be adequately explained only if there was some preface about the unique origins of the church and its positioning as deeply Christian but neither Catholic nor Protestant. He agreed that I could include such a preface, so I went to work.

The article I sent him was published in a book called *Encounters With Eternity*. It is reprinted here as an appendix because, as I think of the gifts of the restoration, there is no greater gift than the knowledge of who we are, where we came from, how we are related to God, and what our possibilities are following this life.

Too often the stunningly beautiful and hauntingly *familiar* questions are "wrapped up" in the difficult and unfamiliar "package" of a church organization and culture with origins and practices that onlookers don't understand.

I believe that this article is an unwrapped version of the gift and thus an appropriate appendix for *The Wrappings and the Gifts*. It follows:

THE CHURCH OF JESUS CHRIST
OF LATTER-DAY SAINTS
by Richard Eyre

While we are often called "Mormons," members of The Church of Jesus Christ of Latter-day Saints know that the full name of our church is both more accurate and more descriptive of the distinctive claim made by the faith. The claim is that there are three organizational categories of Christian churches in the world: (1) Catholic, (2) Protestant (which came about as a result of a reformation), and (3) The Church of Jesus Christ of Latter-day Saints, which is, as the name suggests, the original Church of Jesus Christ, lost from the earth through the middle ages (the *dark* ages), and now restored by God in modern or "latter" times.

Mormons then, agree with Protestants that there was a great apostasy through which many of the "plain and precious" parts of Christ's gospel, along with His authority or Priesthood, were lost. However, unlike Protestants, Mormons believe that more than a *reformation* by men was required to reconstitute Christ's church once it was lost. They believe it required an actual *restoration* by God.

In this context, Joseph Smith was not a reformer, or even the Church's founder. Rather, he was a messenger or a prophet called by God to be a vehicle or conduit through which things that were lost from the world could be restored. The process of truth being lost from the world and then being returned by God has occurred frequently in scripture. Enoch, Noah, Abraham, and Moses — each was a prophet to whom a separate dispensation or restoration of truth was given. While He lived on the earth, Christ himself again restored truth after it was lost. A great apostasy followed the death of Christ and His apostles. Rome first persecuted Christianity, then adopted it, making it a religion of politics and pageantry. In the process, doctrines were changed and compromised and the true authority of God was taken from the earth. The Dark Ages that followed are aptly named. The *renaissance* and *reformation* then opened men's minds and prepared the world for the *restoration* that God brought about through His prophet Joseph Smith, beginning in the year 1820.

Mormons believe in living prophets and think that it is illogical and inconsistent to believe that a just and loving God called prophets

anciently but does not do so today when our need for truth and
guidance is as great as it has ever been. When Joseph Smith was
killed by a mob, Brigham Young, leader of the Church's twelve
apostles, became the second prophet-president of the Church.
Mormons believe that this chain continued unbroken and that there is
a living prophet on the earth today.

Thus the restoration that occurred through Joseph Smith is
consistent both with sacred history and with the world's ongoing need
for living prophets. Many of the great reformers who preceded Joseph
Smith recognized this need. Calvin, Wesley, Luther, and Roger
Williams, among others, indicated that they, while doing all they
could to *reform* Christianity, were awaiting a more complete *restoration* by God himself. Mormons simply believe that this awaited
restoration did occur, and that it occurred through the prophet Joseph
Smith, beginning in 1820 when he prayed for guidance and received
a vision of God the Father and Jesus Christ, who told him that the
original Church of Jesus Christ would be reconstituted in these latter
times.

The things that were restored might be put into three categories:
(1) Accurate doctrine or information about the nature of God and
man, and about where we came from, why we are here, and where we
are going after death; (2) the Priesthood or true authority of God; (3)
additional scripture and ancient records which support and enhance
the Holy Bible and lend further clarification to our knowledge of
Christ and His gospel.

Let us deal with these three categories in reverse order so we can
end with the main subject matter of this article, which is the Mormon
belief in eternity and in life after death.

ADDITIONAL SCRIPTURE

Joseph Smith was directed by God, through an angel, to a set of
ancient records, inscribed in a form of hieroglyphics on thin sheets of
gold, which contained the religious and secular history of earlier
inhabitants of the American continents. This record was called *The
Book of Mormon*, named after a man who collected and abridged the
thousand-year history of his people.

The record, which Joseph Smith was empowered to translate, tells of a man named Lehi, an Israelite, who left Jerusalem about 600 B.C. and crossed the sea with a small group of people, landing somewhere in Central America. A long succession of different generations of writers then give their accounts of their period of history. The people of *The Book of Mormon*, who are some of the ancestors of the modern American Indians, passed through many cycles of righteousness and wickedness. They had among them, at times, prophets of the Lord who taught God's commandments and who prophesied the coming of Christ.

In perhaps the most important and fascinating part of the book, an account is given of the coming of Jesus Christ to the Americas. Immediately following His crucifixion and resurrection, He descended from Heaven to the people of this hemisphere, taught them His gospel, called apostles and established His church and told them that they were the "other sheep" whom he had told His followers in Palestine He must also visit (as recorded in John's Gospel).*

The teachings of *The Book of Mormon* complement and, in some cases, clarify those of the *Bible*. Mormons view *The Book of Mormon* as a "fifth gospel" — as a further witness of Christ and of His divinity. The subtitle of the book is "Another Testament of Jesus Christ." They use the book hand-in-hand with the *Bible* and believe that it is, in fact, the "stick of Joseph" that Ezekiel spoke of and prophesied would become "one in thine hand" with the stick of Judah (the *Bible*).**

Mormons believe that Christ was and is the Savior of the entire world and that it is therefore logical that He visited more than one small part of the earth. He said that He had come to the whole House of Israel. The people in the Americas, having come originally from Jerusalem, were of the House of Israel.

The nickname "Mormon" of course, comes from the belief of The Church of Jesus Christ of Latter-day Saints in *The Book of Mormon*. Additionally, Mormons use two smaller books of scripture called *The*

---

*John 10:16
**Ezekiel 37:15-17

Doctrine and Covenants and *The Pearl of Great Price*. These books contain additional revelations received by Joseph Smith.

PRIESTHOOD OR AUTHORITY

Mormons believe that ordinances like baptism for the remission of sins and the laying on of hands for the gift of the Holy Ghost must be done with the true priesthood or power of God to be effectual. Part of the restoration was the returning of this priesthood to the earth. God sent Peter, James, and John, Christ's three chief apostles, back to the earth as angelic messengers. They laid their hands on the head of Joseph Smith and an associate, Oliver Cowdery, and gave them the authority by which they could perform God's ordinances and once again organize His church. This organization consisted of twelve apostles, of bishops, elders, teachers, deacons, pastors, and evangelists — indeed, of the exact organization that Christ established His original church (see Eph. 4:11-13).

The Church of Jesus Christ of Latter-day Saints was officially organized in 1830. Since then it has become the fastest growing Christian church in the world and today includes over ten million members, slightly more of them living outside the U.S. than in. When nineteen years of age, most young men in the Church elect to serve a voluntary, unpaid "mission" for the Church. They are called to go somewhere in the world (very often where they must learn a foreign language) for two years and preach the Gospel of Jesus Christ to whomever will listen. Young women in the Church also often serve missions.

Mormons believe that the "fruits" of the Church of Jesus Christ (fast growth, low divorce rate, longer life expectancy, high level of education, efficient worldwide welfare system, etc.) are testaments of the truth of the restored gospel (see Matt. 7:16).

DOCTRINE AND INSIGHT (PARTICULARLY ABOUT THE NATURE OF GOD AND MAN)

In his first vision, Joseph Smith relearned much of what man once knew but had forgotten about God. He learned that God the Father and Jesus Christ, His son, are separate and distinct individuals. He learned that they both have glorified, tangible bodies of flesh and bone and that man is literally created in their image. He learned that they are one in purpose, in spirit, and in testimony and witness. They are one in the same way that they desire us to be one with them (see John 17:11, 21).

Some time after the organization of The Church of Jesus Christ of Latter-day Saints, Joseph Smith was asked to summarize the fundamental beliefs of the Church. He did so in what is called the "Articles of Faith":

Article 1:   We believe in God, the Eternal Father, and in His Son, Jesus Christ, and in the Holy Ghost.

Article 2:   We believe that man will be punished for their own sins, and not for Adam's transgression.

Article 3:   We believe that through the Atonement of Christ, all mankind may be saved, by obedience to the laws and ordinances of the Gospel.

Article 4:   We believe that the first principles and ordinances of the Gospel are: First, Faith in the Lord Jesus Christ; second, Repentance; third, Baptism by immersion for the remission of sins; fourth, Laying on of hands for the gift of the Holy Ghost.

Article 5:   We believe that a man must be called of God, by prophecy, and by the laying on of hands by those who are in authority to preach the Gospel and administer in the ordinances thereof.

Article 6:   We believe in the same organization that existed in the Primitive Church, namely, apostles, prophets, pastors, teachers, evangelists, and so forth.

Article 7:   We believe in the gift of tongues, prophecy, revelation, visions, healing, interpretation of tongues, and so forth.

Article 8:   We believe the *Bible* to be the word of God as far
                as it is translated correctly, we also believe *The
                Book of Mormon* to be the word of God.

Article 9:   We believe all that god has revealed, all that He
                does now reveal, and we believe that He will yet
                reveal many great and important things pertaining
                to the Kingdom of God.

Article 10:   We believe in the literal gathering of Israel and in
                the restoration of the Ten Tribes; that Zion (the
                New Jerusalem) will be built upon the American
                continent; that Christ will reign personally upon
                the earth; and, that the earth will be renewed and
                receive its paradisiacal glory.

Article 11:   We claim the privilege of worshiping Almighty
                God according to the dictates of our own
                conscience, and allow all men the same privilege.

Article 12:   We believe in being subject to kings, presidents,
                rulers, magistrates, in obeying, honoring and
                sustaining the law.

Article 13:   We believe in being honest, true, chaste,
                benevolent, virtuous, and in doing good to all
                men; indeed, we may say that we follow the
                admonition of Paul — we believe all things, we
                hope all things, we have endured many things and
                hope to be able to endure all things. If there is
                anything virtuous, lovely, or of good report or
                praiseworthy, we seek after these things.

                                                    —Joseph Smith

Through the process of the restoration, both in his translation of
The Book of Mormon and through other visions and revelations he
received, Joseph Smith learned more of the nature of God and man
and of the answers to the three key questions of the ages: Where did
we come from? Why are we here? And where are we going?

The most concise and clear overview of these questions and their answers that I know of is provided in a beautiful and personal essay by a modern-day apostle named Richard L. Evans. The essay was written as the sound track for a film called "Man's Search for Happiness." It is quoted by permission here:

Sometimes, in your search for happiness you ponder the meaning of your life.

You sift your memory for beginnings; you send your mind ahead for directions, but all you really know is how. And you are lost in the present.

Who am I? How did I come to be? Time — where does it take me? Toward death? And then what? *Who am I?* Where did I come from?

To understand why you are here, you must first understand your beginnings. At birth you did not suddenly flare into existence out of nowhere. You have always lived.

In pre-earth life you were with your Heavenly Father. There, as His spirit sons and daughters, you lived until you were ready to come to earth.

Upon entering mortal life, the memory of your life before birth was blotted out that you might live by faith and further prepare for the everlastingness of life.

This mortal body in which your spirit now dwells is subject to pain, to difficulties, to death. For it is through opposition that you grow in strength of character. You must know pain to appreciate well-being, difficulties to develop courage, death to understand eternal life.

You then, whoever you are, are related not only to every person upon this earth who lives, who will yet live, but to God, the Father of us all, and to His son, our Savior.

With your acceptance of the responsibility of earth life, you were given a wondrous mortal body in the likeness of God.

'So God created man in His own image; in the image of God created He him. Male and female created He them.'[*]

'And the spirit and the body are the soul of man.'[**]

As sons and daughters of God, is it any wonder that *you* are an eternal part of His plan and purpose? And coming from such a noble heritage, that you have possibilities far beyond your greatest dreams?

Be assured that your personal search for happiness has real purpose. Be assured that your life is worth living.

Life offers you two precious gifts — one is time, the other freedom of choice, then freedom to buy with your time what you will. You are free to exchange your allotment of time for thrills.

You may trade it for base desires . . .

You may invest it in greed . . .

You may purchase with it vanity . . .

You may spend your time in pursuit of material things . . .

Yours is the freedom to choose. But these are no bargains, for in them you find no lasting satisfaction.

Every day, every hour, every minute of your span of mortal years must sometime be accounted for. And it is in *this* life that you walk by faith and prove yourself able to choose good over evil, right over wrong, enduring happiness over mere amusement. And your eternal reward will be according to your choosing.

A prophet of God has said: 'Men are that they might have joy'[***] — a joy that includes a fullness of life, a life dedicated to

---

[*] Genesis 1:27
[**] *Doctrine and Covenants* 88:15
[***] 2 Nephi 2:25 — *Book of Mormon*

service, to love and harmony in the home, and the fruits of honest toil — an acceptance of the Gospel of Jesus Christ — of its requirements and commandments.

Only in these will you find true happiness, the happiness which doesn't fade with the lights and the music and the crowds.

God has placed you on earth without memory of your premortal past, but he hasn't left you without hope or without faith in life after death.

This He has promised you: 'I am the resurrection and the life; he that believeth in me, though he were dead, yet shall he live.'*

One of the best attested facts of sacred history is the resurrection of the Lord Jesus Christ. Three days following His crucifixion the disciples were gathered together as recorded in scripture.

> Then the same day at evening, being the first day of the week, when the doors were shut where the disciples were assembled . . . came Jesus and stood in the midst, and saith unto them, 'Peace be unto you.'
>
> And when he had so said, He showed them His hands and His side. Then were the disciples glad, when they saw the Lord.**

Just as you lived before mortal birth, just as you now live in this life, so through the love and sacrifice of your Savior do you continue to live after death.

Like every member of the human race, you were born and you must die. Your birth is a matter of record — you take it for granted. But death, that uncertain door that leads ahead, has been for man an awesome mystery.

Life's greatest test comes with the death of a loved one, and without faith in the immortality of the soul, the separation of death comes forever comfortless.

---

*John 11:25
**John 21:19

After death, though your mortal body lies in the earth, you — your spirit self — being eternal — continue to live. Your memory of this life will remain with you, and the knowledge of your life before birth will be restored.

Like coming out of a darkened room into the light, through death you will emerge into a place of reawakening and find loved ones waiting to welcome you.

There with your loved ones you will await the resurrection, which is the reuniting of your spirit and your body. There you will continue toward the limitless opportunities of everlasting life.

So here you are on earth, with no memory of what went before, and only faith to whisper what comes after.

Be assured that you are here, not by accident or chance, but as part of a glorious everlasting plan.

By a still, small voice within you and through revelation to His appointed prophets, God our Eternal Father guides the affairs of His children.

Today as in the past.

In 1830 God re-established His Church and restored the fullness of the Gospel once more among men through a modern prophet . . .

Joseph Smith.

By revelation our Savior made known again the plan of salvation and exaltation.

Salvation comes as a gift to every man through Jesus the Christ, but *exaltation*, which is the highest of eternal opportunities, you must earn.

It is not enough just to believe in Jesus Christ. You must work and learn, search and pray, repent and improve, know His laws and live them.

This is the way to peace and happiness and the fulness of everlasting life. It is your Heavenly Father's way.

Life Before Birth

Mormons do not believe in a "one-way eternity." They believe that there is a "forever backward" as well as a "forever forward." This believe, however, should not be confused with reincarnation. We believe that we have always lived, but always as *ourselves*, never as someone else or in another life-form. We do not pass from one identity to another. Rather, we remain ourselves and pass through one place and phase of existence after another. We lived with our Heavenly Father who, as part of His plan for our growth and happiness, created this earth for us and, much as a wise father who sends his children to a fine school, allowed us to come here and become more like Him through the process of being tested, gaining physical bodies, and becoming parents and having families of our own.

In the premortal existence before any of God's children had come to live on this earth, God's plan for our growth through agency and self-choice was presented to us all by the Firstborn Spirit of our Heavenly Father who was Jehovah or Jesus. The plan, which allowed mortal mistakes, was made workable by Jesus' willingness to perform His atoning sacrifice. Lucifer, another spirit-leader, presented an alternative to this plan which offered man coercion rather than freedom, and which conferred upon Lucifer the glory and power. He offered it to us as a guarantee that none would be lost, that we would all return. One-third of the hosts of heaven followed Lucifer, who became Satan, and who tempts man today and tries to lead us away from God.

The understanding of our life before birth is a good example of a doctrine that was taught by earlier prophets, but which was distorted and lost during the apostasy. The *Bible* contains many references to our earlier spiritual life (see Jer. 1:5, John 17:3, John 3:13, Job 38:7, Eph. 1:4, Eccl. 12:7), but the references are vague and oblique enough that they have been ignored or misinterpreted. It is points like this that were clarified by the additional scripture and revelation given through Joseph Smith.

Belief in a premortal existence is important for many reasons. It helps explain the feeling of "deja vu" that all experience — and the longings we feel and our sensation that there is more "in us" than just the results of this one short mortal life. It helps us believe in the fairness and justice of God over the course of eternity, even though we see great inequality here and now on this earth. But most importantly, our belief in a premortal existence helps us better understand why we are here, and how this life ties in with God's eternal plan for His children.

Plan Of Salvation

This mortal life is a portion of God's plan for the salvation and exaltation of His children. The experiences and choices we face here present us with opportunities for growth and learning that make us more like God.

Life After Death

When this life ends, our spirits leave our physical bodies and we go to a post-earthly spirit world where we continue to grow and progress and where we await the resurrection and judgment. In this spirit world, all people who have not had an opportunity to hear the full Gospel of Christ receive that chance. As recorded by Peter, this is the place that Christ went to preach to those who had lived during the wicked time of Noah and therefore had no opportunity to know of the true God and His laws.*

Those spirits who accept Christ and His Gospel in the spirit world can receive the same blessings, even the blessing of baptism, as those who accept the Gospel in mortality. Since baptism is an earthly ordinance involving water, it is done by proxy by someone on this earth for and in behalf of one who has died and is in the spirit world. This "baptism for the dead" is referred to in the New Testament** and is God's way of "linking" people, particularly families, with each other by allowing the living to perform works of love for their ancestors and others who died without knowing of the full

---

*I Peter 3:18-19, 1 Peter 4:6.
**I Corinthians 15:29.

Gospel of Christ. This proxy baptism would not be effective for a spirit who did not accept the Gospel in the spirit world.

These vicarious works are performed in the temples of the church and are one reason for Mormons' intense interest in genealogy. Spirits who accept the full gospel in the spirit world but do not have a descendent on earth who is baptized for them will have this work done during the millennium, the 1,000-year period in which Christ will reign personally on earth after His second coming.

The resurrection (a literal physical resurrection of *all* men) will continue with the Lord's second coming in connection with the judgment. This will be essentially a self-judgment, with each person going to dwell with those who are most like him or to where he is most comfortable. Those who have been obedient to God and valiant in their belief in Christ will be comfortable in living with God and will dwell with Him in the Celestial Kingdom.

Mormons believe in the three general divisions of heaven that Paul describes in Corinthians. The highest "degree of glory" (the Celestial) is compared with the sun. The second degree (Terrestrial) is compared to the moon, and the third level (Telestial) is compared to the stars.* All three are kingdoms of glory, and the principal punishment of those in the lower degree will be the regret and realization of what they could have done. The only persons who will not participate in any of the three degrees of heaven will be those who received a sure knowledge and then willfully sinned against the Holy Ghost by rejecting it. This relatively small number will be in outer darkness, becoming numbered among Satan's followers.

Within the highest or "Celestial" degree of glory there will be a "highest level" where families will continue. Thus, in Mormon temples, marriages are performed not until "death do you part" but "for time and all eternity." The eternal nature of marriage and the family is a fundamental belief among Mormons and is partly responsible for the strong family orientation of the church.

Civil marriage (or "until death do you part" marriages) are recognized as legal by the church, but "celestial marriage" performed

---

*Ibid., pp. 40-42.

in the Temple is seen as preferable because it binds families together beyond the grave.

The continuation of marriage and family relationships after death is seen as important, not only because of the happiness and joy it will bring to individuals but because it allows people to be more like God himself who is our *Father* in Heaven and thus continues to be surrounded by His family.

In connection with their belief in "eternal progression," Mormons believe that, as they progress, they become gradually more and more *like God . . . like* their Heavenly Father. This belief (in a loving and personal Father God who wants his children to progress toward what He is) is not unique among Mormons. Dr. Scott Peck, in his best-selling book *The Road Less Traveled*, concludes that "all of us who postulate a loving God, come to a single terrifying idea — God wants us to become Himself. We are growing toward Godhood."*

While many individuals share this view, the Church of Jesus Christ of Latter-day Saints may be the only church that carries an official doctrinal belief in a God who desires that we become as He is. Mormons view God as a loving Heavenly Father who wants His children, in the distant eternities, to become gods themselves.

Funerals, in the context of eternal families' eternal progression are sad in the sense of the departure of a loved one, but *happy* in the sense that that person is with God and that those left behind can someday join him there. Funeral services usually dwell on the comforting and reassuring of those left behind with the conviction that it is we on the earth who suffer the most grief, not the departed spirit who is now continuing on his or her journey of eternal progression.

The Birth That We Call Death

To further clarify and elaborate the Mormon belief in life after death, let me, for the balance of this essay, quote selectively from a

---

*M. Scott Peck, *The Road Less Traveled*, N.Y., NY: (Simon & Schuster, 1978), p. 269.

book I co-authored called *The Birth That We Call Death.** In it I quote extensively from priesthood authorities in the Mormon Church:

When a loved one has passed on, two kinds of comfort are available. One comes with condolence and love of friends, the soothing words of poet and philosopher, and the comforting presence of the Holy Spirit.

The other lies in knowledge and insight — knowledge of where the loved one is and insight into what he is doing.

Through revelation to his appointed prophets, our Heavenly Father has given us this knowledge. Because of his love for us and his understanding of our need for comfort, he has told us with positive clarity and strong assurance where our loved ones go.

By studying God's revealed word, we can be sure of six things:

1. That the spirits of all men, immediately upon death, go to a spirit world to await the resurrection.

2. That, for the righteous, the spirit world is a place of joy and peace.

3. That it is also a place of continued progress and a place of missionary work, where those who have received the gospel can teach it to those who have not.

4. That our departed loved ones are changed only in that they are temporarily separated from their physical bodies; that in personality, character, and characteristics they remain the same; that the spirit does not change.

5. That the spirit world is not far removed from us but close by, though invisible to our mortal eyes.

6. That some departed spirits know and understand our thoughts and feelings; that they are aware of us and retain their love for us.

---

*Richard M. Eyre and Paul H. Dunn, *The Birth That We Call Death*, (Salt Lake City), Utah, Bookcraft, Inc. 1976.

The following statements of prophets give us this knowledge and assurance. Note how positive and precise they are, how specific and complete they are.

> Behold, it has been made known unto me by an angel, that the spirits of all men, as soon as they are departed from this mortal body, yea, the spirits of all men, whether they be good or evil, are taken home to that God who gave them life. And then shall it come to pass, that the spirits of those who are righteous are received into a state of happiness, which is called paradise, a state of rest, a state of peace, where they shall rest from all their troubles and from all care, and sorrow.[*]

> When the spirits leave their bodies they are in the presence of our Father and God; they are prepared then to see, hear and understand spiritual things. But where is the spirit world? It is incorporated within this celestial system. Can you see it with your natural eyes? No. Can you see spirits in this room? No. Suppose the Lord should touch your eyes that you might see, could you then see the spirits? Yes, as plainly as you now see bodies, as did the servant of Elijah. If the Lord would permit it, and it was his will that it should be done, you could see the spirits that have departed from this world, as plainly as you now see bodies with your natural eyes.[**]
>
> — Brigham Young

> The spirits of the just are exalted to a greater and more glorious work; hence they are blessed in their departure to the world of spirits. Enveloped in flaming fire, they are not far from us, and know and understand our thoughts, feelings, and motions, and are often pained therewith.[***]
>
> — Joseph Smith

---

[*] Alma 40:11-12, *The Book of Mormon.*
[**] Eyre and Dunn, op. cit., p. 27.
[***] Ibid., p.27.

When a person who has always been good and faithful to his
God lays down his body in the dust, his spirit will remain the
same in the spirit world. It is not the body that has control over
the spirit, as to is disposition, but it is the spirit that controls the
body. When the spirit leaves the body, the body becomes
lifeless. The spirit has not changed one single particle of itself
by leaving the body.*

— Heber C. Kimball

Imagine for a moment that you are about to cross the country on
a train. You get on board, and as the train starts you find yourself
sitting next to a fine person who is making the same journey that you
are. Since the trip usually takes almost four days, you begin a serious
attempt to get to know each other. You find that you have much in
common, and by the time the train steams into the darkness at the end
of the first day, you feel a remarkable closeness and begin to feel that
the relationship you are forming may be the most important part of
your journey.

After a sound night's sleep in the Pullman car, you rejoin your
friend and the two of you spend another day relating to each other and
experiencing the journey together. Your rapport grows still stronger,
and you find yourself feeling a little sorry that the day passes so fast.
By the second night your train is deep into the flat middle plains, and
as you fall asleep you are thinking about the things you want to find
out and talk about with your friend the next day.

In the morning you return to your seat and find, to your dismay,
that your friend is gone. When you inquire, someone tells you that he
got off during the night. Got off during the night? But he had a
destination very near your own, and you had planned on having the
next two days with him, and there was so much more left to say!
Suddenly you realize that you never did find out quite where he came
from or just who he really was, and that you never did learn why he
was on the train or exactly where he was going. Worst of all, you

---

*Eyre and Dunn, op. cit., p. 27.

realize that you don't know whether you'll see him again — that you don't know how to find him or contact him.

The feeling is a mixture of sadness and frustration which together produce something in between bitterness and anger. Why did he have to leave? Did someone or something make him leave? Should you be upset at him for leaving or at someone else who made him go against his will? It's not so much that he's gone, it's that you don't know *where* he's gone and you want so much to see him again.

At that point the porter comes down the row to your seat. The message he leaves is very simple, but it changes night into day and bitterness into joy. He tells you that your friend was indeed going to the same place as you — that he was going there to see his father. During the night the train received an emergency message which instructed your friend to get off the train at the next stop and catch a plane to get home more quickly, because his father needed him right then. The porter leaves you a phone number so that you can contact your friend as soon as you arrive.

The simple message of the porter turns your frustration into peace. You are still sorry to miss the two days of discussion you had anticipated with your friend, but your sorrow is no longer bitter or blind; rather, it is sweet with the knowledge of where he is and the assurance that you will see him again.

The sorrow we taste with the loss of a loved one can be bitter or sweet, depending on one ingredient — the ingredient of knowledge — the simple, pure knowledge of our origin, our purpose, and our destination. The restored gospel gives us this knowledge. It tells us our origin; it reveals our purposes on earth; and it teaches us of the life hereafter, assuring us that loved ones will meet us there and that death is a temporary separation and not an utter loss.

As in the imaginary journey on the train, the sense of temporary separation that comes to one who knows the plan of salvation does not carry the sting and panic of permanent loss.

Benjamin Franklin once said:

> Our friend and we were invited abroad. . . . His chair was ready first, and he is gone before us. We could not all conveniently

start together; and why should you and I be grieved at this, since we are soon to follow, and know where to find him.*

Any dear possession, if separated from us for good purpose, and if returned in even better condition, produces joy rather than agony and peace rather than frustration.

One man loses his billfold containing a large sum of money. Another, with the same amount, sets goals and makes a planned investment. Both are now separated from their money, but one feels the bite and bitterness of permanent loss, while the other anticipates the day when he will retrieve his investment and enjoys the knowledge that it will probably grow in the meantime.

A loss we cannot comprehend or accept (and a loss that is considered permanent) is bleak and stark and comfortless; but a temporary separation is a part of a goal and plan is acceptable and, in a way, even joyful. The loss of a loved one — the parting of the spirit from the physical body — is not a permanent loss, neither is it a separation we cannot accept or comprehend. Rather it is indeed an indispensable part of the goal and plan of God.

In the comprehension of the goal and plan of God lies true and lasting comfort and the ability to view death as *The Book of Mormon* Prophet Jacob did: ". . . Death hath passed upon all men, to fulfill the merciful plan of that great creator. . . ."**

God is the literal father of our spirits, and Christ the Firstborn, is our eldest spirit brother. We stood with them in the pre-earthly existence and may have heard our Father state his goal: "For behold, this is my work and my glory, to bring to pass the immortality and eternal life of man."***

God the Father had achieved immortality and eternal life in a perfected, resurrected body. His goal was that we should become like him. As an infinitely wise father he had achieved ultimate joy, and as

---

*Eyre & Dunn, op. cit., p. 33.
**2 Nephi 9:6, *The Book of Mormon.*
***Moses 1:39, *The Pearl of Great Price.*

an infinitely good father he wanted us to become like him and thus to share that joy.

In that pre-earthly existence there were three broad differences between ourselves and our spirit Father, differences that had to be overcome if his plan were to be fulfilled and we were to become like him. First, God had a body, a glorified, perfected physical body that gave him certain capacities that we did not have. Second, he had power and intelligence and knowledge far beyond ours. Third, he was perfect and had great characteristics that we had not.

We realized, as he did, that we could begin to overcome these differences only through the experience of a mortal existence on a physical earth. This realization and the prospect of gaining physical bodies and experiencing earth life, aroused within us such gratitude and elation that, according to the Old Testament, we and all the hosts of heaven "shouted for joy."* There in the pre-earthly existence we must have had certain insights that we lack now, insights into the great value of earth experience and into the importance of that experience in God's plan of eternal progress.

We anticipate the joy of being able to relate to both spiritual and material things. We knew we needed physical bodies to feel with, to learn with, to react with.

Having defined both his goal (that we should become like him) and the vehicle for that goal (a physical earth), God ordained a plan, a plan that would bring about his goal, a plan for the salvation of his children.

Another direction was presented — by Lucifer, sometimes called a son of the morning. It must have had the appealing, safe sound of a guarantee, for Lucifer's promise was, that he would redeem all mankind, that not one soul could be lost. Apparently he would do this through coercion, making sure we all did what was necessary for salvation. Hence his plan contained no opportunity for failure nor for growth and development. And all he asked for himself was everything — the full credit, the whole glory.

---

*Job 38:7.

While Lucifer's power-play was rejected, the Father's plan was wholeheartedly accepted by Jehovah (Jesus Christ), the Firstborn. It called for agency and initiative. It included free choice and the opportunity for both success and failure. Because of its freedom, the plan offered the possibility of pleasure but also of pain, of virtue but also vice.

Because it was realistic, it anticipated sin and error which, unatoned for, would permanently separate men from God. Thus Jehovah offered to be that atoner, to come to earth himself, to gain a physical body and, as Jesus Christ the Only Begotten Son of the Father, to willingly sacrifice his life for the redemption of the world.

As spirits we realized that through the operation of this great plan of salvation Adam would fall, bringing spiritual death and physical death (mortality) upon mankind. Jesus Christ would atone for Adam's transgression so that, in Paul's terminology, just as all men would die, all would subsequently be made alive,* and thus physical death and physical resurrection would become two automatic transitions in eternity. Christ's atonement would also be, in John's words, the propitiation** or payment for everyone's sins so that, as we would repent, those sins could be removed, thus allowing us to overcome spiritual death as well as physical death.

There is much comfort in the knowledge of a "forever backward" as there is in a "forever forward." Knowing where a loved one came from, why he was here, and that he achieved the basic purpose of his earth life, turns death from "the terrible unknown" to a necessary step in the attainment of an immortal body and in the achievement of our eternal goal.

If, in the premortal existence, we looked forward to birth, which was the leaving of our Father and our eternal family, how much more we must have looked forward to death, which would be a later and essential step in the coming home!

Mortality is the prerequisite to immortality; it is by passing the tests and gaining the progress of this world that men obtain eternal

---

*I Corinthians 15:22.
**I John 2:2.

life. Thus death (passing from time into eternity) is as important and as wonderful as birth (passing from eternity into time), and both are among the essential transitions in the Father's plan for our salvation.

Brigham Young said:

> There is no period known to them (the dead) in which they experienced so much joy as when they pass through the portals of death, and enter upon the glorious change of the spirit world.*

On this earth we view death from the perspective of one who stays behind, much as a man views a long journey when he is sending someone else off rather than going himself. He puts his friend on the train or plane and waves good-bye, only able to imagine what the trip is like and what the friend will find when he gets where he is going.

If we could glimpse, for even a moment, the glory and excitement that a departed one faces when his eyes close on time and open on eternity — if only we could glimpse this, perhaps there would be more understanding in our sorrow and more joy in our grief.

We know almost enough, through scriptures and revelation, to imagine what death's awakening may be like. Lift yourself for a moment from your own shoes and into the role of one who is departing from this earth. You close your eyes for the last time on the sights of this world and become aware that you are being pulled and lifted up and out and away from your physical body. You feel somehow lighter, perhaps both in weight and in illumination. Your eyes, this time spiritual eyes, now become open, and you are aware that you see and hear and feel and sense things which were closed to you while on earth.

Because you somehow have powers you lacked before, you can see the realm of spirits which you now enter. You recognize some of those you see. There is great rejoicing as they reach out and you embrace in the light of love and peace. You already miss your physical body, and somehow you now understand its importance, but

---

*Eyre & Dunn, op. cit., p. 53.

you know it will be returned to you in the resurrection; and so you go forth meeting and remembering those you knew before.

Joseph F. Smith said:

> . . . Those from whom we have to part here, we will meet again and see as they are. We will meet the same identical being that we associated with here in the flesh. . . . Deformity will be removed; defects will be eliminated, and men and women shall attain to the perfection of their spirits, to the perfection that God designed in the beginning.*

Brigham Young said:

> We cling to our Mother Earth and dislike to have any of her children leave us. . . . But could we have knowledge and see into eternity, if we were perfectly free from weakness, blindness and lethargy with which we are clothed in the flesh, we should have no disposition to weep or mourn. . . . It is true it is grievous to part with our friends. We are creatures of passion, of sympathy, of love. . . . Should we not . . . rejoice at the departure of those whose whole lives have been devoted to doing good. . .?**

Thus, we know that the spirits of all men, as soon as death occurs, go directly to the spirit world where they await the resurrection, the final redemption and the judgment. As *The Book of Mormon* Prophet Alma says, "There must needs be a space betwixt the time of death and the time of the resurrection."***

In general terms the spirit world, to which all spirits go at death, is divided into the abode of the righteous (paradise) and that of the wicked.**** After his death, the Savior bridged the gulf between them

---

* Ibid., p. 54.
** Ibid., p. 55
*** Alma 40:6, *The Book of Mormon.*
**** Alma 40:11-14, *The Book of Mormon.*

by bringing the gospel to the spirits in prison.* Since that time, righteous spirits have been called to minister and teach the gospel to those who did not have it on this earth. Thus the spirit world is a place where those who had no opportunity to hear and accept the gospel on earth will have that opportunity, so that they can "be judged according to men in the flesh, but live according to God in the spirit."**

It has been said that all truly deep and meaningful happiness stems from one of two sources: (1) service, helping, and giving to others; and (2) anticipation, looking forward to and waiting for something important or fine. If indeed these are the two key sources of joy, the spirit world must offer great potential happiness, because it contains the greatest conceivable opportunity for service and holds in its future the event most worthy of eternal anticipation. A righteous spirit in paradise can teach other spirits the most important and indispensable knowledge in the universe and anticipate the greatest event: the glorious resurrection which makes possible the continuing eternal progression of the righteous.

Speaking of the great service and mission being performed by the righteous in the spirit world, Brigham Young said:

> Compare those inhabitants on the earth who have heard the gospel in our day, with the millions who have never heard it, or had the keys of salvation presented to them, and you will conclude at once as I do, that there is a mighty work to perform in the spirit world.***

If you can imagine the happy anticipation of a boy who has been away at a severe and demanding boarding school and who now returns to the beautiful home of his father whom he loved dearly — if you can imagine that happiness and then magnify it a million times, then perhaps you can glimpse the joy of a righteous spirit awaiting his glorious resurrection.

---

*See I Peter 3:18-21, Moses 7:39, *The Pearl of Great Price; The Doctrine and Covenants*, Section 138.
**I Peter 4:6.
***Eyre & Dunn, op. cit. p. 56.

The joy we anticipate in the spirit world will come into full fruition in the resurrection, when our spirits will reunite with perfected resurrected bodies, our own physical bodies, which we will rejoice in finding again and which will be immortal and incorruptible.

No two facts are more clearly and explicitly stated in sacred scripture than those — the reality of Christ's resurrection and the certainty of ours. The apostles witnessed the wound in Christ's resurrected body and watched him eat the fish and the honeycomb. They went forth testifying, as he had, that, just as all men would die because of Adam, so also all men would live because of Christ.

David O. McKay said:

> If Christ lived after death, so shall men, each one taking the place in the next world for which he is best fitted. Since love is as eternal as life, the message of the resurrection is the most comforting, the most glorifying ever given to man; for when death takes a loved one from us, we can look with assurance into the open grave and say, "He is not here," and "He will rise again."*

In the resurrection the spirit will re-enter its physical body, which initially will be in exactly the same state as when the spirit left it. Bodies that were sick, infirm, or deformed will then be restored to health and perfection, apparently almost instantly — as Amulek says, to a "proper and perfect frame."** Nor will he at time of death determine a resurrected being's appearance. Joseph Fielding Smith said:

> Old people will not look old when they come forth from the grave. Scars will be removed. No one will be bent or wrinkled. . . . Of course, children who die do not grow in the grave. They will come forth with their bodies as they were laid down, and then they will grow to the full stature of manhood or womanhood after the resurrection, but *all* will have their bodies fully restored.***

---

*Ibid., p.57.
**Alma 1:43, *The Book of Mormon*
***Ibid. pp. 57-58.

   In his supreme wisdom and his sublime love, God has laid out before us a plan of such excitement and such beauty that it is difficult, while in the flesh, to fully comprehend it. As we learn it, though (by outward study of the word and inward study of our souls), we are lifted to higher realms, we face more easily the trials of our lives, and we feel the joy that can go with the sorrow of bereavement.

   The Lord said to the Prophet Joseph Smith, "Wherefore, fear not even unto death; for in this world your joy is not full, but in me your joy is full."*

Doctrine and Covenants 101:36.

BACKGROUND/AUTHOR

To more and more people, **Linda and Richard Eyre** have come to symbolize the most important phenomenon of America in the '90s — the return and recommitment to family life styles and mainstream values.

One of the Eyres' several best-selling co-authored books, *Teaching Your Children Values* is the first parenting book in 50 years to reach #1 on the "New York times" best-seller list. They have also advocated strong families and balanced life styles in major national media, ranging from *Oprah* and *Donahue* to *CBS This Morning* and *Today* and from the *Washington Post* to *USA Today*. They host the national weekly cable TV show *Families Are Forever* and two national satellite TV shows: *Lifebalance* and *Teaching Children Values*. They founded (and run) the international parents' cooperative organization, *HOMEBASE*, which includes nearly 100,000 parents throughout the world, and were named by President Reagan to direct the *'80s White House Conference on Children and Parents*.

Richard and Linda have nine children (one of every kind) and live in Washington, D.C. and Salt Lake City. The Eyre children are increasingly involved in what the family calls "Eyrealm." Two daughters work as managers at The Points of Light (national volunteer coordinating) Foundation. Five of the children have interrupted their college to live abroad, working in orphanages or doing other humanitarian and voluntary service work. The younger children, still living at home, have each written parts of the Eyres' books and frequently participate with their parents in media appearances and in seminars, particularly for *The Disney Institute* in Orlando and for the *Young Presidents Organization* throughout the world.

With degrees from Utah State, Brigham Young, and Harvard Universities, Richard is a management and political consultant, who has had clients ranging from Nelson Rockefeller to Lord Grade of London. He ran for governor in 1992 and served on the President's Advisory Panel for Elementary and Secondary Education.

OTHER BOOKS*

by Richard and/or Linda Eyre

Lifebalance
Spiritual Serendipity
Spiritual Stewardship
Spiritual Synergy
3 Steps to a Strong Family
The Awakening (a novel)
What Manner of Man/The Secret of the Sabbath
Children's Stories to Teach Joy
Teaching Your Children Values
Teaching Your Children Joy
Teaching Your Children Responsibility
Don't Just Do Something, Sit There
I Didn't Plan to be a Witch

*If you have trouble finding any of these titles, order direct by calling (801) 581-0112.

RICHARD M. EYRE

THE
SECOND RINGS

A short book of
spiritual connections

ISBN 1-55517-303-9

PREFACE

For nearly 20 years, with virtually every manuscript Linda and I delivered to our publishers (Random House and Simon & Schuster), we would have a predictable session with our editors who would politely ask us if we couldn't try a little harder to avoid the use of spiritual terminology and inference. "We publish to broad, mainstream audiences," they would say, "and we have to be careful not to offend anyone." We would dutifully re-edit our books, trying to make the spiritual references (which we refused to take out) more subtle.

Then, in the mid-'90s, something changed. America became less apologetic about its spirituality, and strong currents of "soul and spirit" became evident within the "mainstream." Our editors (those same editors) started saying to us, "Can you get a little more spirituality into your next books?" We were happy to oblige — because we have always felt that if we possess any unique writing talent, it lies in taking what we believe in our souls and putting it into words that ring true to the hearts of others.

So, Simon & Schuster is now publishing (to its mainstream) a trilogy of deeply and overtly spiritual books of mine called *Spiritual Serendipity, Spiritual Stewardship,* and *Spiritual Synergy.*

But there is an interesting (and in some ways tragic) dichotomy in the public mind between "spiritual" and "religious." Religion still, to so many, suggests dogma, bureaucracy, and overly simplistic, non-satisfying "explanations." For me, the dichotomy does not exist. My spirituality and my religion are one. The feelings of my spirit and the teachings of my church are consistent and congruent with each other. That is why I felt the need to write this book . . . to have something to offer those who like the answers and insights of the trilogy and who ask, "Where do those insights come from?"

They come from the doctrine of the restored Gospel of Jesus Christ. May you find joy and peace in that *source* as well as in His *light*.

Richard Eyre
Jerusalem, 1996

P.S. One final (and important) preface thought: Please do not misunderstand the intended purpose of this book. It is not written to convince you or convert you to my beliefs. *Spiritual conversion*, as the term implies, comes only by and from the Spirit — it is not an intellectual process — it has more to do with what we call the heart than with the mind.

My hope for this book (both sides of it) is that it will arouse enough interest to prompt readers to *pursue* the Spirit's influence through prayer, through listening to those called as missionaries, and through reading books that are more than books — The Holy Scriptures.

The reasoning of this book will not give inner conviction to your spirit, but it will, hopefully, point you toward spiritual sources that will.

CONTENTS

INTRODUCTIONS

This is an introduction and an *explanation* of the second rings . . . of what they are and of what they can do.

It is perhaps more important than most introductions, because the *content* of the rings cannot be discussed until the rings themselves are defined, identified and appreciated.

Thus three introductions are offered, one for the poetic and intuitive right brain, one for the logical and deductive left brain, and one for the metaphorical brain that exists somewhere in between.

Right Brain Introduction

"My wish is simple," I cried.
"I want to be happy and I want to give
happiness
to those I love."

From somewhere deep within
(or maybe from someone far without
and high above — I could not tell)
came a still answer:
You must believe.
You must become.
You must belong.

I knew that identity and purpose were the heart
of my prayer for happiness and
I came to feel,
mostly in the solitude of starry nights
or on mountain walks, alone, that
believing and *becoming* and *belonging*
were the answers
to the happiness question.

But they were do-it-yourself answers,
conceptually complete but not integrated or implemented.
They were compass directions on a half-drawn map,
partial blueprints not yet built.

I believed in a God I did not know
and in a spirit within myself
that I could not always find.
I believed that the latter one came somehow from the former
but I did not know how or when or why.
I needed a link, a second ring, to connect the two.

I had plans for short-term success
and dreams of some long-term heaven.
But I wondered if one worked against
the other.

I wanted to achieve and succeed
but in quiet hours I knew there was somewhere a
guidance
that was better than goals.
I needed another second ring between.

I was a father and a citizen.
I had family and state,
but I was running one and being run by the other.
I needed help with one, a buffer from the other,
a nurturing second ring with family inside
and society outside.

The big and the little,
The close and the far
are easier to see than what's in between.
The connecting links,
the second rings
are harder to find, to grasp, to accept;
but they are what
completes us
and pulls us to where enduring happiness
is within reach.

Left Brain Introduction

It has been said that happiness depends on *believing, becoming,* and *belonging.* And whether or not one accepts the happiness premise, it is clear that much of our personal identity and self-image rests on what we believe in, what we belong to, and what we are striving to become.

Both identity and happiness are undermined by doubts, voids, and inconsistencies in what we believe, by the loneliness and isolation of not belonging, and by a lack of clarity and commitment in what we want to become.

Interestingly and ironically, with all three of the "B" words, most people are strong and clear on the macro and on the micro but weak and unclear on how to connect the two:

*Believing:*Most believe in God and most believe in some sort of spirit within themselves which continues after death . . . yet most have little clarity or security about the *relationship* of their spirit to God. They lack the second ring or the link between themselves and God and thus the most important questions become imponderable — "Who am I?" "Where did I come from?"

Becoming: Most have strong ideas about (and strong desires for) what constitutes success in the here and now — for what they want to do and to become. And most believe in some sort of heaven or afterlife as the ultimate destination. But most people have a hard time *connecting* the two. They lack the second ring or the link between present efforts and eternal rewards and thus cannot find answers for the pivital questions: "Why am I here?" and "Where am I going?"

Belonging: Most belong to a family and consider their family a part of a town or city, a state, and a nation, but few have a nurturing neighborhood or an identity-expanding group that is bigger than family but smaller than the whole community. They lack the second ring or connecting link between household and larger society. Thus they have a hard time with questions like: "Where and how do I get the help I need?" and "Where and how do I give the help I need to give?"

The biggest problem about our believing, our becoming, and our belonging, and the biggest barricade to our happiness is that we are *disconnected* . . . many of the best and truest parts of our convictions, our identities, and our purposes are weakened and isolated because the links that could activate and energize them are missing.

The single, simple purpose of this book is to help you find the missing second rings — and make the connections that can complete your believing, your becoming, and your belonging, allowing them to be navigable passages to happiness.

Metaphorical Introduction

1. *Believing*

Within the human race, substantial majorities believe in a God and nearly equal numbers believe they have within them a spirit that lives on after death.

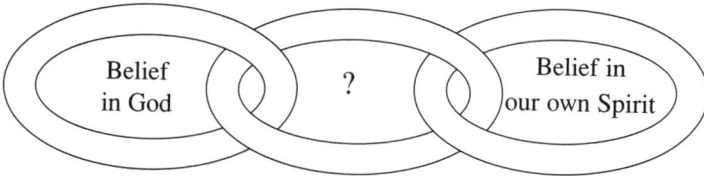

But both beliefs are limited in the power and effect they can have on people unless they are linked by some belief in the *relationship* between the two. How are we related to God? Why do we call Him Father? Who are we to Him? Did we come from Him? Is He involved in our everyday lives? How do we access Him and His guidance?

If we are the micro (our own small individual selves) and God is the macro (the creator and master of all), then what is between? What is the connection and the tie that makes each relevant to the other? What is the second ring?

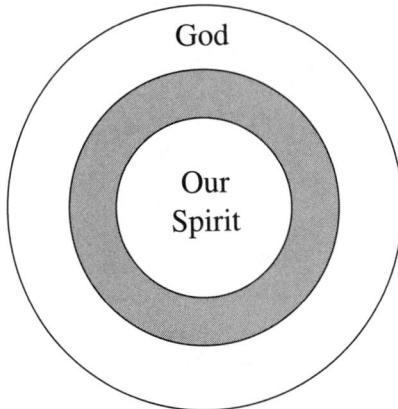

2. *Becoming*

We are all motivated on some level to progress, to move forward, to achieve our own definition of success. Virtually everyone seeks *improvement* of some sort.

And "heaven" or some form of eternal, after life destination is an almost universal belief.

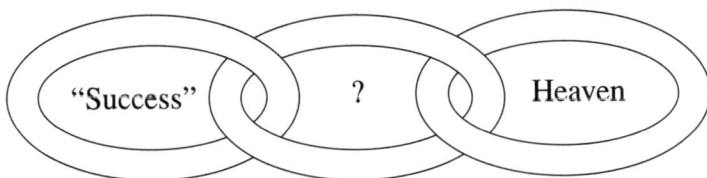

But there is little meaning in our achievements here unless they provide longer-range joy and lead to some more ultimate destination. Indeed, we can only guess at what success is until we see connections to something further away and more absolute. Short-range goals are ultimately meaningless unless they lead to longer-range goals. What is the *purpose* of life? Why are we here? How do the experiences of mortality affect and interrelate with eternity? What really matters and what really doesn't? Is there a point or a purpose to pain, to failure, to heartache?

Again, if we see the close, the micro, the personal and if we believe in the far, the macro, the eternal, what is in between? What connects one to the other? What makes one relevant to the other? What is the second ring?

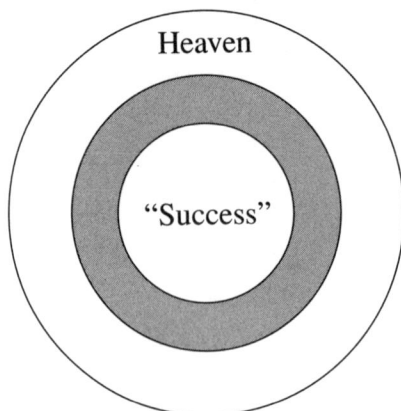

3. *Belonging*

Everyone needs to belong. The sentiment is so universal it has become a cliche´. "No man is an island."

Belonging used to be easier than it is today. Families and extended families were stronger, neighborhoods and communities were more coherent and nurturing. People stayed longer and had more sense of place and more identity with something bigger than self.

Today virtually everyone is still a part of some kind of family and we all live in a state or nation, most of us in a city or town. What has really disintegrated is the link between.

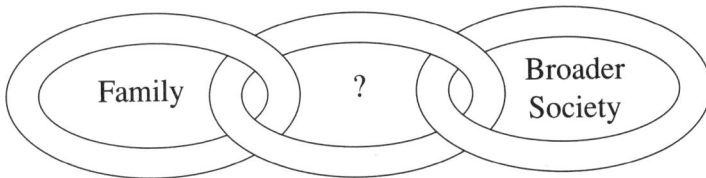

The most basic unit of society (the family) used to be pretty well supported and linked to broader society by a close knit neighborhood, or by an active local community, or best of all (because it gave spiritual as well as temporal unity), by a community church that was both involved and involving.

Families (and individuals) need help and support from a source that is closer and more intimate than the state or the municipal government. People need to belong to something bigger than their immediate family yet much smaller than their city or town. We need an identity and commonality bigger than ourselves, and we need practical as well as believable answers to questions like: Where do I get personal help when I need it? Who will support and reinforce the values I'm trying to teach my kids? Where and how can I give meaningful help to others? Who will back up the beliefs I have and teach me the ones I need?

The micro family can neither give to or get from the macro society unless there is a nurturing, supportive, effective interphase. What can it be? What can give us the security of being bigger than ourselves? What can teach us and support us and strengthen and expand our identity? What is the second ring?

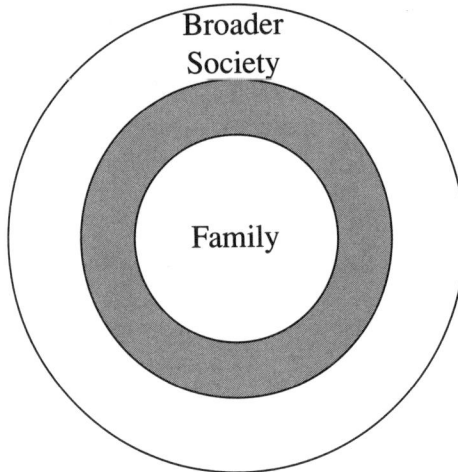

Connecting and Strengthening

If they can be found, the missing second rings don't only *connect* the inner and outer, they *strengthen* them as well.

The "believing" second ring should not only accurately explain our relationship to God, it should clarify who and what God is and reveal to us the deeper identities of our own souls.

The "becoming" second ring, in addition to giving longer-term purpose to our goals and efforts, should also redefine what "success" really is and clarify what heaven is and how we can get there.

The "becoming" second ring, besides connecting our families to broader society, should support and strengthen our families, help us as parents, and reinforce our beliefs and convictions and provide ways for us to both give to and receive from the society in which we live.

Do these magical, connecting second rings really exist? They do!

Do we create them or search for them? Search! (Because they already exist and they come from God.)

Where do we look? For starters, in this book. Then beyond.

THE SECOND RINGS

The lost second rings have a Divine Source. Little effort will be made here to prove that is so, because the content of the rings is self-testifying. That is, as the content of each ring is expressed (bluntly, boldly, without hedge, qualification or justification), it carries its own "light of insight" or "ring of truth" so that your spirit will recognize (almost *remember*) it and be able to accept it without "proof."

After giving you the rings this book will conclude with how they were restored.

BELIEVING

The ring connecting our belief in God and our belief in the spirit within us.

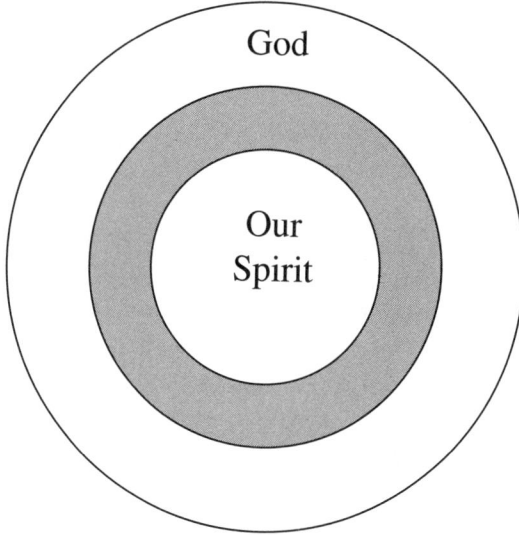

God exists.

An eternal spirit exists within each person.

The connection between them is the most beautiful and the most basic relationships in the universe. We are *children* of God. God is our *Father*. We, all of us on earth, are literal, spiritual brothers and sisters.

At birth, we did not suddenly flare into existence. The feelings of deja vu and of echos we sense of an identity older and deeper than our physical bodies are *true*. They are not suggestions of reincarnation or other lives as other people. They are traces of memory from our earlier spiritual lives when we lived with God and prepared to come to this earth.

This earth is a phase in our eternal existence, a "grade" or level in our eternal education and growth toward God our

Father. God made the earth, this incredible miraculous orbiting school, for us. It contains every option, every opposite, every obstacle and every opportunity necessary for our learning, our progress, our discovery of personal destiny. God, as any wise Father sending a child off to college, knew we needed space, agency and independence to continue our progression.

In our pre-earth life, we were presented with an eternally relevant decision or choice between two alternative plans for mortality. One leader in that world offered a plan in which he would guarantee our return to God. He promised to remove the risk of failure in return for personal glory and honor for himself. The other leader presented a plan of freedom and agency . . . and risk. We would choose our course. Many would give up their right to return through mistakes that severed them from God. He would sacrifice himself to atone for those mistakes allowing additional chances (but no guarantees) for our return to God.

One-third of God's children followed Satan and his false guarantee, forfeiting forever their mortal opportunity. Two-thirds, including you and me, followed Christ.

Our relationship to God is that of a father and a child. We are His spirit children. Our spiritual selves had form and were recognizable. We looked like ourselves. Spirit is matter — more refined than the matter we now know. We lived with God. We knew Him as our Father. He knew us individually as His children. Our ultimately wise and loving Father then gave us the ultimate gift — a physical body on a physical earth where we can, through new experience and adversity, mature spiritually in ways that make us more like Him. Here we give physical birth to others of His children, assuming the honor and the title *parent*, which previously belonged only to Him.

Here, our memory of our first home is blocked (though not always entirely) by a spiritual veil so that we can develop faith and have the agency and independence necessary for true growth and progress.

This second ring (of our relationship to God) *activates* the inner and outer rings of our belief. The God we now believe in is our parent. The spirit we now believe in is God's off-spring. In this context, prayer becomes personal. Spiritual confidence, generated by our younger sibling relationship to Christ, grows in parallel with the increased humility that stems from our dependence on His atonement.

BELIEVING *is* a key to happiness, but we must believe not only in God and in the eternal spirit within men . . . we must also find belief in the relationship between the two, the relationship that can return the one to the other.

BECOMING

The ring connecting our desire for "success" and our desire for heaven.

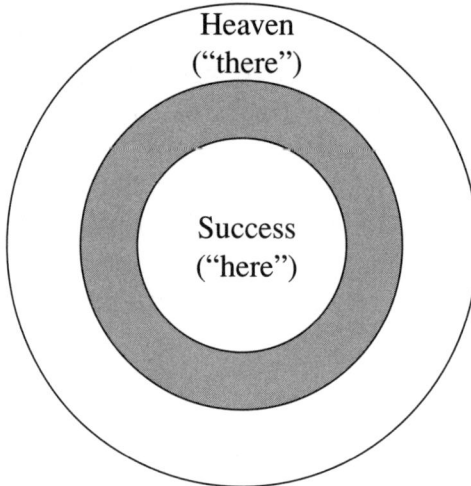

Life does continue after death.

And our lives here affect our lives there.

Built into us all is a desire for progress, for growth, for achievement, for "success." And the missing second ring is God's own plan of "eternal progression" — of spiritual growth that will allow us to return to Him and to be more like Him than when we left His presence to come to this earth.

By definition, since God is perfect, omnipotent and omniscient, all true progress, learning or growth that we undergo here makes us — ever so slightly — more like Him. Because of his perfect love for us, He wants us to have what He has and be what He is. This earth is a step in His plan to bring that about.

All of the beauty, and opportunity, and kindness and love that exist in the world is part of His gift and His plan. And what looks to our limited perspective like pain, ugliness, and arbitrary unfairness, looks, in His broader and longer view, like the alternatives and opposites necessary for the growth and development we came here to find.

By gaining earthly bodies we experience physical and emotional feelings previously not available to us . . . feelings and emotions that stretch our souls and expand our awareness and our empathy.

By becoming parents we discover a deeper and more selfless form of love and commitment than we were capable of before.

By encountering pain and doubt and failure we discover our strength and resilience, we develop character, and when we reach the end of our capacity, we can develop the dependence on God which creates humility and qualifies us to feel His spirit and receive His guidance.

By forming families we form the beginnings of our own tiny kingdoms, and we develop bonds of the deepest love which will carry over into eternity and become the structure of the organization of Heaven.

By striving to overcome appetites of selfishness, greed, and indulgence, and through efforts to live by true principles and values, we gradually gain the independent strength of spirit that can qualify us to return to God and to participate in His kind of happiness.

By repenting and improving, we avail ourselves of the forgiveness and fresh start made possible by Christ's atonement, and by baptism we symbolize this cleansing and commit ourselves to follow His example and serve within His church.

The families we form here can be eternal. In Christ's church, marriage vows say "for time and for all eternity" rather than "'till death do us part." We return to God as families — an embryonic microcosm of His eternal family.

The transitional event that we call death is really more of a birth — a rebirth back into our true home. We leave our bodies here and go to a spirit world where progress continues. Those who did not experience Christ and His gospel here have those opportunities there. Choice still exists and over the course of God's plan all have equal opportunity to determine who they will be and who they will follow.

The luminance of this second ring — of God's plan for our eternal life — lights and redefines the beliefs we already had about "success" and about heaven.

Success, in this new context, is no longer about wealth or station or comfort or competition. It is about giving and growing, about character and concern, about love and the inner life.

And heaven, understood through Christ's gospel and God's plan is anything but the cliche´ of endless rest on fluffy clouds. It is a realm of continued progress, of expanded awareness, of unfolding joy.

Priorities, simply defined, are the things that matter most in eternity — our families, our character, our service to others, the love and joy we develop and carry in our hearts.

BECOMING *is* a key to happiness, but we need to refine our aspirations so that what we prioritize matches with God's plan and fulfills us *here* even as it fulfills His requirements for *there*.

BELONGING

The ring connecting our families and the broader society.

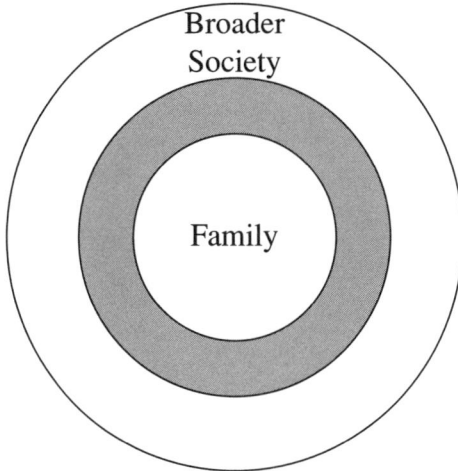

Some things are too big and some are too small,.

Our families are the most important things we belong to, but they are often too small to give us all the associations we need or the temporal or spiritual help we may need or to try to protect us from every negative influence or to help us with the difficulties we're having within our families themselves.

We all also belong to a society — we are citizens of our town or city or state. But these are too large and too impersonal to nurture us spiritually, to reach out to us personally, to become part of our identity and to enhance our scope of self.

We need a second ring, a middle level, a close, neighborhood group to which we can belong, from which we can draw help, comfort, understanding, concern and stimulation; and to which and through which we can give of ourselves.

To some extent a company or a workplace can be this second ring. We often have an expanded identity through our work along with many personal associations. Sometimes clubs and fraternities meet part of the need; and though it is becoming more rare, some neighborhoods or community centers play this role. But the emphasis of the company is economic, the club is recreation, and the community is civic.

People need a second ring where the emphasis is *personal* and *spiritual*. People need the second ring of a church.

The Lord's church is His kingdom upon this earth, but it is also a local, personal location and congregation that involves individuals, fortifies families, gives and receives service, teaches and trains, includes people and expands identities.

The Church of Jesus Christ has individual congregations called wards, each headed by a local, lay minister called a Bishop and his two counselors. All three are volunteers, unpaid, working in an ordinary job — as are all of the teachers, youth leaders, and organization leaders and workers within the ward. Almost everyone has a "church job" so members essentially serve each other and support each other's families. Each ward has a scouting program, and athletic, music and drama programs, and various service organizations so that the local ward building or church is in use virtually every evening.

Wards are not exclusive but inclusive with non-church members invited to meetings and activities as well as members. Service is rendered in the neighborhood to members and nonmembers alike.

With all of its involvements and activities, the *principal* function of the ward is to teach the Gospel of Jesus Christ. On Sundays and on at least one week night, members (adult and youth) are able to go to classes and study the Gospel through the scriptures. Daily, early morning "seminary" classes are available to adolescents and teens in most wards.

Shared convictions and similar priories create the potential for very close personal relationships within wards. The congregation is often referred to as the "ward family" and really is a secondary and supplemental family for its members.

When an individual or family experiences illness or accident or other need, the ward is there to offer assistance and encouragement. When someone is out of work or experiencing economic difficulty, the ward provides the opportunity for short-term welfare work whereby food and basic necessities are *earned*. When marriages and families have problems, counseling and assistance are available.

Ward members look out for each other's children and for each other's property. Ward members are assigned by the Bishop to be home teachers and home visitors and to look in on each family at least once a month and to deliver help where it is needed.

The second ring of a local church is important not only to *give* us the help and assistance and identity we need but also to provide effective vehicles and channels whereby we can help others.

Our basic need to give help to others, to contribute, to be needed is as strong as any need we have to receive help. The "callings," the church jobs, the service projects that are integral parts of a ward fulfill our needs to give and organizes and orchestrates what we can give so it is effective and meaningful to those who receive it.

BELONGING is probably the most recognized of all human needs and the most accepted requirement for happiness. Nothing is as important as belonging to a family, but that is not enough, and belonging to a society is too distant and too impersonal to be meaningful. *Belonging* to Christ's church, and to our own local congregation of that church can include us, instruct us, involve us, and inspire us to *become* all that we can be and to *believe* all that is true.

POSTSCRIPT

In the words of a child . . . the profound simplicity of the Restoration.

How were the second rings of Believing, Becoming, and Belonging lost? And how were they restored?

One way to answer these questions would be an exhaustive review of secular and religious history — an answer comprising the Roman persecution of Christianity, the divisions and subsequent compromises within the church, the Dark Ages and the barbarism of competing factions, the Reformation and the compelling efforts to rediscover and re-establish lost truth and lost authority, the restoration of truth in a last and final dispensation of Christ's Gospel.

But this detail is the content of other books. This book will answer the questions in the refreshing and somehow deeply fulfilling words of a six-year old child.

I was driving one Sunday evening along a winding road in Southern England, on my way to make a speech about our church to a group of interested "investigators." Traveling with me, along for the ride and the chance to be together, was my six-year-old daughter Saren.

To pass the time, and to help focus my mind on what I might say in my speech, I began asking questions to Saren.

"Honey, why do you think Jesus came to the earth?"

Saren, who had been going to school in England for two years and acquired a perfect and proper British accent (along with a delightful British articulateness and ability to come right to the point) thought for a moment and said:

"I suppose He came to teach us how to be nice and to show us how it is going to work when we die."

We rode in silence for a few minutes while I pondered her answer. Given the same question, I would have gone on about the Gospel and the resurrection and all the inferences and implications of both. But a six-year old could say it all in one sentence, ". . . to teach us to be nice and to show us how it is going to work when we die."

I decided to see what other wisdom I could draw out of her. "Was there any other reason why He came? What else did He do while He was here?"

"Well," said Saren, "He set up a proper church."

The British get a lot of mileage from the word "proper." It means right, correct, as it should be, everything in order, complete, whole. Saren had found the perfect, one-word description for the church that Christ established on this earth.

I went on. "What happened to the proper church after Jesus was crucified?"

Saren thought for a while on this one but then gave another one sentence answer. "Pretty soon the Apostles got killed, too, and the church got a bit muddled."

"Muddled." Another descriptive British word — confused, disconnected, at odds with itself, divided, unclear, imprecise. Countless volumes have been written about the apostasy within Christ's church, about its poticalization as the Church of Rome, about the factions and divisions, about doctrinal change and evolution, about councils and attempts to compromise and re-unite . . . but Saren summarized it graphically. "The Church got a bit muddled."

There was an obvious next question: "So what did Jesus do about the muddled church?"

This time Saren 's was immediate. "Well, He came back down to a prophet and He put it right."

"Put it right" the British say. Correct, renew, restore. That was what I would speak on later that night. That Christ had returned to a prophet. That He had restored the parts of His pure, precious gospel that had been lost. That he had re-

revealed the answers to our questions of who we are, where we come from, why we are here, where we are going. That He had given back the missing "second rings" that could reconnect our lives and our faith, that He had *put it right*.

FOR FURTHER INFORMATION

Even after (maybe especially after) reading both sides of this book, you may have further questions. Probably the best way to get them answered is to call the "Mormon" church nearest you (listed as The Church of Jesus Christ of Latter-day Saints). That will get you in touch with two young Mormon missionaries who will try — humbly and honestly — to tell you more personally about the church, and to answer your questions.

If *we* can be of help in any way — through others of our books — or anything we might send you on parenting, on values, or on "lifebalance," please call us or our staff at (801) 581-0112.

All the best,
Richard and Linda Eyre